BIBLE
Comes to Life

Book 3
REDEMPTION

Joy Sukadi | Lilyana Margaretha

BIBLE COMES TO LIFE

BOOK 3: REDEMPTION

© 2025 by Joy Sukadi and Lilyana Margaretha

All rights reserved. No part of this book may be reproduced in any form without permission in writing from the publisher, except in the case of brief quotations embodied in critical articles or reviews.

Unless otherwise indicated, all Scripture quotations are taken from the Holy Bible, New Living Translation, copyright © 1996, 2004, 2015 by Tyndale House Foundation. Used by permission of Tyndale House Publishers, Inc., Carol Stream, Illinois 60188. All rights reserved.

Scripture quotations marked NIV are taken from the Holy Bible, New International Version®, NIV®. Copyright © 1973, 1978, 1984, 2011 by Biblica, Inc.® Used by permission. All rights reserved worldwide.

Scripture quotations marked NIrV are taken from the Holy Bible, New International Reader's Version®, NIrV®. Copyright © 1995, 1996, 1998, 2014 by Biblica, Inc.® Used by permission of Zondervan. All rights reserved worldwide. www.zondervan.com. The "NIrV" and "New International Reader's Version" are trademarks registered in the United States Patent and Trademark Office by Biblica, INC.TM

Scripture quotations marked CEV are taken from the Holy Bible, Contemporary English Version. Copyright © 1995 by American Bible Society.

All emphasis in Scripture has been added.

Editor: Pam Lagomarsino and Sara Boyd

Illustrations: Natalia Wijaya and Lilyana Margaretha

Interior and Cover Design: Rachdian Topasca and Juliana Lemong

Cover Image: Kreker Kate

A list of photo/image credits is at the end of this book.

ISBN: 978-1-7376802-2-2

Published by Sharpening Little Arrows, LLC
Mill Creek, WA 98012
www.sharpeninglittlearrows.com
E-mail: sharpeninglittlearrows@gmail.com

Welcome to Bible Comes to Life! 5

Introduction 10

Quick Start Guide... 11

Material List... 12

3-1: The Greatest Gift 14

3-2: Amazing Grace 28

3-3: Jesus Christ: Fact or Fiction 46

3-4: Jesus Christ: Fully God, Fully Man 68

3-5: The Cross: Fact or Fiction? 84

3-6: Jesus' Resurrection: Fact or Fiction?.................... 102

3-7: Holy Spirit: Our God and Helper.......................... 120

Truth Blast! 138

Notes 142

Photo Credits 145

About The Authors 146

Welcome to Bible Comes to Life!

"Equipping Children with Biblical Truths to Challenge Cultural Lies"

DEAR FRIENDS,

Our journey started in 2019 as our children were elementary school age. We observed the world around us and noticed we are raising our children in a different day and age now. They are bombarded daily with a progressive agenda, lies, perversity, and skewed truth through media, school indoctrination, perverse library books, and more. This simple question filled our hearts: how do we equip our children to stand strong against popular beliefs and cultural lies? The current is strong; the pressure is great. We heard so many stories of kids with Christian upbringing turn away from their faith once they go to college (or even earlier!).

During that discouraging time, God spoke clearly in our hearts: **"Daughters, you cannot stop the flood from coming, but you can start building an ark for your family—intentionally and with a purpose. Your family will be saved!"** We could not stop the non-biblical culture from bombarding our children, but we could win this battle by equipping them from the inside out! In this saturated "woke" culture, sending our children to Sunday schools, youth groups, or summer Bible camps will not be enough anymore. Discipleship and equipping need to happen every day, in our homes, by the closest people raising them—*us!* The Word of God in Psalm 127:4 (NIV) resonated loud and clear in our hearts:

> *"Like arrows in the hands of a warrior are children born in one's youth."*

As parents, we are called to shape our next generation so they can be as sharp as arrows. We are assigned to raise sons and daughters of clarity who can detect the enemy's lies from hundreds of miles away. We must equip them daily with biblical truths so they can push back the darkness and defend the truth. The Bible tells us in 1 Peter 3:15:

> *"Instead, you must worship Christ as Lord of your life. And if someone asks about your hope as a believer, always be ready to explain it."*

In creating this "Bible Comes to Life" series, we hope and pray we will equip our children in a logical way so they can boldly defend their faith as they grow up. Here you will find resources to do intentional discipleship in the heart of your homes. This series will help you instill biblical values and teach solid apologetics truths to your children in **relevant and engaging** ways. The best part of all: we use SCIENCE and logical explanations to support the biblical truth. We know children are highly visual with short attention spans. Their curious minds respond best to *exciting games, science experiments, arts and crafts, and compelling story-telling from their parents.* Even Jesus talks in parables.

With constant streams of games and entertainment surrounding our children, the Bible could become an archaic and irrelevant resource for them if we are not careful. Our vision is to bring the Bible to life again in our children's hearts by presenting God's Word in the most exciting, creative ways. We want kids to experience, taste, and see how real and magnificent our Creator is.

We designed this book series **for busy families** like yours and mine. It is filled with **fundamental biblical values to impart**. In each lesson, we compare a non-biblical worldview and a biblical worldview. We then support the biblical values with an *activity, experiment, arts and crafts, or other methods* to make the Bible relevant. The activities are so simple that you can find materials in your kitchen or a short trip to the craft store. Each lesson will take about thirty to forty-five minutes. Lessons can also promote fun family time on the weekends, during summer vacation when children are not in school, or even during the busiest weeknights!

Finally, at the end of each lesson, you will find intriguing questions to foster a meaningful family discussion. This time provides opportunities for you, parents, to open up about your past, tell heartfelt stories, and "download" unforgettable truths into your children's hearts. It basically kills two birds with one stone: **creating a strong bond within your family while also building a solid biblical foundation in your children's lives.** See this book as your eternal investment to launch your children into the world prepared and ready to defend their Christian faith. We are excited to be on this journey with you!

For our children's souls,
Joy and Lilyana

Book 3

Redemption

For this is how God loved the world:
He gave his one and only Son, so that everyone who believes in him
will not perish but have eternal life.

John 3:16

Introduction

. . .

As parents, waiting is a constant part of our lives. Yet, no matter how often we experience it, it never seems to get easier. Whether we're longing for milestones, healing, breakthroughs, or the salvations of our loved ones, waiting can feel heavy. Let's take a moment today and reflect:

What is the one thing I'm really waiting for today?

(Think of something that fills our prayers, brings us to tears, and occupies our thoughts in this season.)

For centuries, God's people waited for the promised Messiah. Then, in the fullness of time, God ended that wait by sending His one and only Son. This was the ultimate sacrifice—the fulfillment of a promise made thousands of years earlier. Jesus, the promised Savior, was born as a baby, just as prophesied after the fall.

As we journey through the Scriptures, we see that God was never idle during those years of waiting. He was actively orchestrating every detail, preparing for His perfect plan of salvation to unfold at just the right time.

Through the lessons in this book, we will discover **God's unwavering faithfulness** as the ultimate **Promise-Keeper**. He doesn't just make promises—He fulfills them! He never forgets His promises, and His heart has always been set on us. He also understands the weight of our waiting and the ache of our longing.

Yet as we wait on God, our focus and perspective shift. We begin to see that no matter what we're waiting for, ultimately, it's **Who** we're waiting on that matters most. Waiting isn't passive—it strengthens our faith as we trust God to act in His perfect timing. And if God is for us, who can be against us? (Romans 8:31). Let's begin!

Quick Start Guide

We know you are eager to jump into the lessons. But before you do, here are a few important things to note.

Each chapter contains a lesson ready to be read aloud by the parent(s). In each lesson, you will find:

- Purpose
- Icebreaker (either questions or a mini-game)
- Introduction
- Non-biblical View
- Biblical View
- Activity (including materials and instructions): science experiments, engineering, or other hands-on activities.
- Discussion
- Summary
- Truth to Remember
- Memory Verse
- Fact Check

The **Activity** sections serve as a guideline for parents. While most materials can be found easily at home, we recommend checking the Activity section a few days before the lesson to ensure you have everything prepared.

In the **Discussion** sections, expected answers for certain questions are provided in parentheses. Some questions also include additional read-aloud sections to reinforce key truths and help children make meaningful connections after sharing their answers.

At the end of each lesson, you'll find a **Fact Check** section designed for parents and older children to explore Scripture, scientific and historical insights, and other valuable resources in greater depth.

For a quick reference and a deeper understanding of how each lesson connects to the big picture, visit the **Truth Blast!** section at the end of this book. This section compiles key biblical truths and verses from all the lessons, making it a handy tool to review as you progress.

Lastly, be sure to check out additional resources, including videos and articles, on our website:
www.sharpeninglittlearrows.com

Material List

As promised, we want to make it as easy as possible for you to use this book. So, we put together a list of all materials you will need in the lessons for your quick reference.

3-1: WATER VS. SOAP

- A white (or any light-colored) bowl
- Black pepper
- Water in a small container
- Dish soap in a small container

3-2: PEPPER LIFTING

Note: *You may prepare a dish and spoon for each family member and have everyone try the experiment individually.*

- Pepper
- Salt
- A plastic spoon
- A colored dish
- Dry wool cloth or fur *(or simply rub the spoon on hair)*
- A piece of paper towel

3-3: THE INVISIBLE FORCE

Note: *Using fresh yeast is important in this experiment. If you have yeast that has been stored for some time, test its freshness by following the steps in the lesson.*

- A balloon
- One packet or 2 ¼ teaspoons of dry yeast
- One teaspoon of sugar
- One cup of warm water
- A bowl
- A funnel or a measuring cup
- A bottle

3-4: HOMEMADE ICE CREAM-IN-A-BAG

- 1/2 cup half-and-half, heavy cream, or non-dairy milk alternatives
- 1 tablespoon sugar
- 1/4 teaspoon vanilla for flavor *(or check the lesson activity page for other flavors.)*
- 3 cups ice
- 1/3 cup rock salt or regular table salt
- Gallon-size sealable plastic zip-style bag(s)
- Quart-size sealable plastic zip-style bag(s)
- Kitchen towel/potholder
- Cold tap water
- A small ice cream bowl
- Optional toppings and mix-ins: sprinkles, chocolate sauce, fruits, crushed Oreo cookies, mini marshmallows
- A music player *(optional)*

3-5: DISAPPEARING SIN

Note: Try the activity beforehand to find which plate and glass combination works best.

- A glass plate with a smooth, flat bottom
- A clear drinking glass or jar
- A penny (or any other coin)
- A votive or tea light candle that fits inside the glass or jar
- Lighter or matches
- A cup of water
- Food coloring

3-6: EXPLODING STICKS CHAIN REACTION

- Jumbo wooden craft sticks (at least 25 pieces)

3-7: PAPER WINDMILL

Note: Your family may make one paper windmill per person, or the whole family can work together to make one windmill. You may make a sample paper windmill before the lesson to show the final product.

- Construction or cardstock paper (or use thin cardboard from an empty cereal box)
- Cardboard tube (from the middle of paper towels, or make one from construction/cardstock paper taped together to form a tube)—one for each windmill
- Straw—one for each windmill
- Pushpin/nail
- Sharp pencil
- Ruler
- Scissors
- String
- Tape
- A small paper/plastic cup or empty yogurt cup (optional)
- Small, light objects that can fit inside the cup, for example, rice grains, paper clips, or small erasers (optional)
- A glass of plain milk *(optional—for discussion)*
- Chocolate syrup *(optional—for discussion)*

3-1
The Greatest Gift

PURPOSE

To show our children that God *freely* gives the gift of salvation through His Son, Jesus Christ.

Icebreaker

- What was the best gift you ever got?
- What makes it memorable to you?

3-1 The Greatest Gift

When we think of Christmas gifts, we might remember the song "Santa Claus is Comin' to Town," which reminds us to be good if we want presents. But the Bible tells us that **no one** is perfectly good (Romans 3:10). For many years, people have been asking questions like:

Will I get in trouble for my mistakes?
What happens after I die?
Can I go to Heaven if I keep making mistakes?
Will I come back as an animal, like a cat, a dog or maybe a cow?

Just like kids try to stay off Santa's "naughty list," people have worked hard to be good so they don't upset powerful beings, like God or other gods. But since everyone makes mistakes, they wonder:

How can I make things right with God?

To find answers, many people turn to **religion**. Religion teaches us about what happens after we die, how to live, and how to worship. There are lots of different religions, and each one has its own answers and ideas.

Did you know there are more than 4,300 different religions in the world?[1] Can you name some of them?

*The most popular ones are Christianity, Islam, Hinduism, Buddhism, Sikhism, and Judaism. (If you want to learn more about these religions and how they are different from Christianity, check out the links in the **Notes** section.[2])*

• • •

17

NON-BIBLICAL VIEW

Each religion has its own way of connecting with the powerful being they believe in. Some religions teach that doing good things can help fix our mistakes and make us accepted by God.

Have you ever seen people bowing down to statues? They believe they have to do that or go to a special place to make themselves "clean." In Japan, some people even do something very extreme—they pray and walk for a thousand days![3] That's a lot of walking!

People think if they try their best to follow the rules and do good things, they'll be okay. Some even mix different religions together to make their own!

Now, can you see what these religions have in common? They all say **we need to do something** to connect with God.

But can we really be good enough to connect with a **holy** God?

BIBLICAL VIEW

The Bible tells us that we all make mistakes and fall short of God's glorious standard (Romans 3:23). Sin is a problem because it breaks our friendship with God and has a **cost**. No matter how hard we try, we can *never* fix it by ourselves. Trying to reach a holy God on our own is impossible!

But God didn't give up on us. When the first people sinned and broke their friendship with God, He had a **big plan** right from the beginning:

God Himself made a special effort to reach out to us.

He sent Jesus—God's own Son—to save us from being separated from Him forever (Genesis 3:15). Jesus died on the cross to pay for our sin. By doing this, He fixed our relationship with God. Now we can be His friends!

Some people still try to get to God on their own, but remember: God is holy, and we can't make ourselves "clean." Only Jesus has the power to do that. Let's do an experiment to help us understand this!

3-1 The Greatest Gift

Activity

Water vs. Soap

MATERIALS

- A white (or any light-colored) bowl
- Black pepper
- Water in a small container
- A teaspoon of dish soap in a small container

INSTRUCTIONS

1. Fill the bowl with about an inch of water.
2. Sprinkle black pepper evenly and carefully across the water surface. The pepper flakes should float, not sink.

3. Dip your finger into the water in a small container.
4. Lightly touch the center of the pepper-sprinkled bowl with your wet finger..

5. Observe what happens to the pepper flakes.
6. Clean and dry your finger.
7. Squeeze 1–2 drops of dish soap into another small container.
8. Ask children:

   "What do you think will happen if you touch the center of the pepper-sprinkled bowl with your soapy finger? Can you guess how the pepper flakes will react?"
9. Dip your index finger lightly into the dish soap.

10. Touch the center of the pepper-sprinkled bowl with your soapy finger.
11. Observe what happens to the pepper flakes.

Discussion

1. In our experiment, let's think about what each thing represents:
   - The water in the bowl is like **our lives.**
   - The pepper flakes are like **our sins.**
   - The water in the small container is like **the things we try to do on our own to get rid of our sins.**

   What happened when we touched the pepper-sprinkled bowl with a finger dipped in water?

   ___

   (**Answer:** *Nothing!*)

   It shows that **when we try to get rid of our sins by ourselves, it doesn't work.**

   (This is an important part of the experiment called the "control." A control is something in an experiment that stays the same or doesn't change, even when other things are different. It helps scientists compare and see what happens when they change something.)

2. What happened when we touched the pepper with a finger dipped in dish soap?

   ___

   (**Answer:** *Most pepper flakes moved away from where we touched them, and some fell to the bottom. It looked like the soap was chasing the pepper flakes away!*)

   The dish soap is like **the blood of Jesus**. When we try to get rid of our sins by ourselves, it doesn't work. But with the power of Jesus, we are made clean and right in God's eyes!

   Ephesians 2:8–9 says:
   > *God saved you by his grace when you believed. And you can't take credit for this; it is **a gift from God**. Salvation is not a reward for the good things we have done, so none of us can boast about it.*

3-1 The Greatest Gift

3. Read together **Romans 3:24–25** (NIrV).

> The **free gift of God's grace** makes us right with him.
> Christ Jesus paid the price to set us free.
>
> God gave Christ as a sacrifice to pay for sins
> through the spilling of his blood.
> So God forgives the sins of those who have faith.
> God did all this to prove that he does what is right.
> He is a God of mercy. So he did not punish for their sins
> the people who lived before Jesus lived.

What is the special gift from God in the Bible verses we just read?

_____

_____

*(**Answer:** It is God's grace that makes us right with Him. It's given to us when Jesus died for us.)*

The blood of Jesus washes away all our sins. He forgives everyone who believes in Him. Instead of punishing us, He gives us the **gift of salvation!**

Salvation is being saved from something bad. In Christianity, it means being saved from the punishment of sins, which is death and being separated from God. Instead, it's like getting a second chance—we get to be close to God and become part of His family forever!

4. How do we get this amazing gift of salvation?

_____

_____

*(**Answer:** We believe that Jesus is the only solution to our sin problem, and we just need to say "yes" to Him. This means we trust Him and let Him be in charge of our lives. He becomes the leader we follow everyday.)*

5. Would you like to receive this free gift of salvation from God? Let's pray together!

(If children are ready and willing to do so, lead them in the following prayer to receive Jesus into their hearts.)

"Dear Lord Jesus, I know I am a sinner, and I ask You to forgive me. I believe You died on the cross for my sins. You rose from the dead, and You are alive today.

I want to turn away from my sins and invite You to be my God. I know I can't save myself; only You can! I want to trust and follow You as my Lord and Savior. In Jesus' name, Amen."

Summary

We can't earn God's special gift by being good or doing things on our own. God gave us this gift **freely** because He loves us so much! When Jesus died for us, He made **a way for us to be close to God**. All we need to do is trust in Jesus and welcome Him into our hearts.

Truth to Remember

My greatest gift is this: Jesus died on the cross to save me from my sins.

… and the blood of Jesus, his Son, cleanses us from all sin.

1 John 1:7

FACT CHECK

THE SCIENCE BEHIND "THE WATER VS. SOAP" EXPERIMENT

In this experiment, we see how soap works to clean things. Do you remember when you sprinkle pepper on water, and it just floats on top? That's because water molecules like to stick together, making a kind of "skin" on the surface called **surface tension**. Since pepper doesn't like water (it's hydrophobic), it sits on top of this skin without sinking.

But when we add soap, something amazing happens! Soap is like a superhero that can break apart this skin made by the water molecules. When soap touches the water, it changes how the water molecules stick together, and the surface tension breaks. This change makes some of the pepper sink, and the rest moves away with the water as it tries to get away from the soap.

So, the next time you wash your hands with soap, remember how it helps break down dirt and germs, just like it does with the pepper in our experiment!

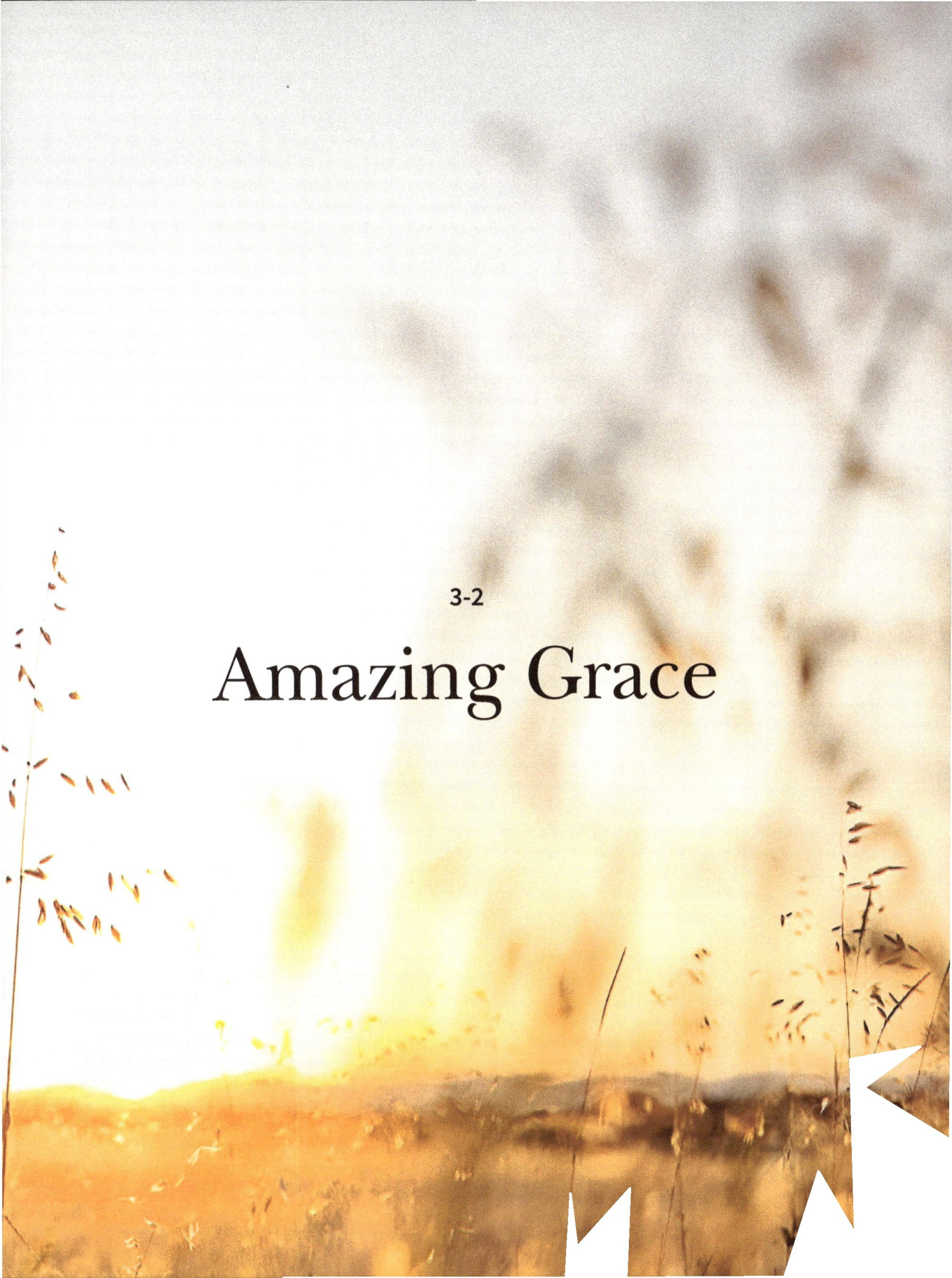

3-2

Amazing Grace

PURPOSE

To learn about accepting God's gift of grace.

Icebreaker

- What is the hardest thing you've ever had to deal with? Was it something at school, with friends, or at home?
- Think about what made it hard and how you handled it. Share your story with your family.

In the last chapter, we talked about a special gift God gave us. Do you remember what it is? God saved us by His **grace** because He loves us so much, not because we did anything to earn it (Ephesians 2:8–9).

Do you know what **grace** means?

Grace is when someone is kind to us or gives us something good, even if we don't deserve it.

Grace is like when you get an ice cream treat even after you get a bad grade. God's grace is a special gift from Him because He loves us so much. He gave us this gift by sending Jesus to take away our sins, even though we didn't deserve it. We can *never* pay Him back for such a wonderful gift! **John 3:16** (NIV) says:

> *For God so loved the world that he gave his one and only Son, that whoever believes in him shall not perish but have eternal life.*

NON-BIBLICAL VIEW

Why do some people say NO to God's free gift of grace? Well, they think it's too good to be true. They might wonder:

> "Why would God give us something for free?"
>
> "What do I have to do in return?"
>
> "What's the catch?"

Some people might say, **"I'm already good enough"** or **"I don't need God."** They believe that as long as they are not doing anything really bad and are doing well in life, they don't need God's grace. But is that true? Is God's grace only for people who make big mistakes? Let's find out!

BIBLICAL VIEW

The Bible tells us that **everyone** needs the grace of God, not just people who do really bad things.

> All people sin and need God's grace and forgiveness.
> Even kids who seem really good are still sinners!

God is perfect and holy, but we are not. **Isaiah 59:2** says our sins have **separated** us from God. Because of sins, we can't be close to God or talk to Him like friends do.

But can you guess why God gives us this gift of grace? Let's find out together in **Ephesians 2:4–5.**

> *But God is so **rich in mercy**, and he **loved us so much**, that even though we were dead because of our sins, he gave us **life** when he raised Christ from the dead.*

Isn't it amazing? God's mercy means He doesn't punish us as we deserve. But wait, there's more!

God loves us so much that He forgives us, makes us right in His eyes, and gives us a new life in Him.

That's what we call **amazing grace!** It's like having a friendship with a perfect God, even though we don't deserve it.

Now, let's dive into an experiment to understand what it really means to accept God's gift of grace.

Activity

Pepper Lifting

MATERIALS

- Pepper
- Salt
- A plastic spoon *(keep it hidden until needed)*
- A colored dish *(a non-white dish would make it easier to see the salt)*
- Dry wool cloth or fur *(or simply rub the spoon on hair)*
- A piece of paper towel *(to contain the removed pepper flakes)*

Note:
You may prepare a dish and spoon for each family member and have everyone try the experiment individually.

INSTRUCTIONS

1. Pour 1 tablespoon of salt onto a dish. Say:

   "We know Jesus died on the cross to cleanse us from our sins."

   *"Now, imagine this salt is your life **after** Jesus became a part of it—a **new life as a Christian.** Let's see what happens next."*

2. Sprinkle pepper on one side of the dish, right on top of the salt. Say:

   "Although we try our best to live like what Jesus wants us to, sometimes we still make mistakes. We might say or do things we shouldn't, not listen to our parents or teachers, or argue with our siblings. Remember, nobody is perfect while we're on Earth."

   *"This pepper is like the **mistakes or sins** we still make, even after we ask Jesus to be a part of our lives."*

3. Sprinkle some more pepper on another side of the dish. Say:

    "We also live in a broken world where a lot of bad things happen. There are sicknesses, natural disasters, and many other tough things."

    *"The pepper on this side is like all the **bad and hard things in life**."*

4. Today's challenge is to separate the pepper from the salt. Ask children:

    "Now here's the challenge: How can we get the pepper away from the salt?" (**Answer:** *You could try using your fingers or a spoon to scoop it up.*)

    "How long do you think it would take to remove the pepper piece by piece with your fingers?"

    "Do you think there's a faster way to separate the pepper from the salt?"

5. Now, let's reveal a hidden secret: the plastic spoon! Take the spoon out and rub it on a dry wool cloth, fur, or your hair about 20-30 times.

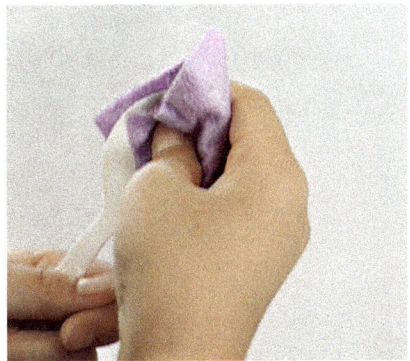

6. Bring the back of the "charged" plastic spoon close to the first pile of pepper. Observe what happens.

7. Use a piece of paper towel to wipe off the pepper stuck on the spoon.
8. Bring the back of the plastic spoon close to the second pile of pepper. Watch what happens.

   Tip: If the spoon doesn't seem to be working, try rubbing it again to "charge" it.

9. Repeat steps 7 and 8. Remove as much pepper as possible.

3-2 Amazing Grace

1. Do you remember what the salt and the two piles of pepper are like? What do you think the spoon represents?

   (Answer:
   - *The salt is like* **our life after we receive Jesus.**
   - *The first pile of pepper is like* **our mistakes or sins.**
   - *The second pile of pepper is like* **the bad things and challenges in this world.**
   - *The spoon represents* **God.***)*

2. As we rubbed the spoon, it built up something called **static electricity**. This invisible force was strong enough to remove the pepper from the salt, just like how God's grace works powerfully in our lives. *(See the **Fact Check** section for the science behind this experiment.)*

   What does God's grace do? Let's think about it with the pepper in our experiment.

   *(**Answer:** God's grace forgives our sins, makes us part of God's family, and gives us strength.)*

   Just like the spoon moved the *first* pile of pepper, God's grace **forgives us** and **takes away our sins.** He also **adopts us into His family.** Instead of just being servants, God calls us His sons and daughters (John 1:12)!

   And just like the spoon moved the *second* pile of pepper, God **gives us the strength to face hard times** and **share His love with others.** When things get tough, we don't have to do it alone. God's grace is always enough. As it says in 2 Corinthians 12:9 (NIV): "My grace is sufficient for you, for my power is made perfect in weakness." So, even when things are hard, we can trust God to help us when we ask Him.

3. Let's talk about an example of God's grace from the Bible. Remember, God's grace is a special gift we don't deserve, but He gives it to us because He loves us. *(Choose **one** of the following examples.)*

- The story of **the Prodigal Son** (Luke 15:11–32):
  A young man asked his father for his inheritance and left home to spend it all. Later, he realized he had made a mistake and decided to go back home. When he returned, his dad welcomed him with love and forgiveness, even though he didn't deserve it.

- The story of **Saul of Tarsus**, who later became known as the apostle Paul (Acts 9:1–30):
  Saul used to hurt and even kill many Jesus' followers. But one day, while he was on his way to harm more Christians, he met Jesus. Saul experienced God's grace in a powerful way, and it completely changed his life. He stopped hurting others, began following Jesus, and became one of His most devoted followers.

These stories remind us that no matter what mistakes we've made or how far we've turned away from God, His grace is always there for us. He loves us unconditionally and is ready to forgive us when we come back to Him.

4. Even though God's grace is always there for us, does that mean we should keep doing things we know are wrong? (**Hint:** Read **Romans 6:1–2**.)

> Well then, should we keep on sinning so that
> God can show us more and more of his wonderful grace?
> Of course not!
> Since we have died to sin,
> how can we continue to live in it?

_____

_____

_____

(**Answer:** *The Bible says we should not.*)

It's like saying, "Since I know Mom will always forgive me, I'll just keep making messes!" But instead, we should try our best to do what's right because we love God. Even though God forgives us, there are still consequences for our actions.

5. What comes next after receiving God's gift of grace? Let's read **Acts 20:24** (NIrV) together.

> But my life means nothing to me.
> My only goal is to finish the race.
> I want to complete the work
> the Lord Jesus has given me.
> He wants me to **tell others about the good news of God's grace**.

So what should we do?

_____

_____

_____

(**Answer:** *We need to share the good news about God's amazing grace with others.*)

6. How can we share God's grace with others?

- **Tell others about Jesus and His gift of grace whenever you can.**

    Remember, God can use anyone—no matter how old or young you are, or what your life looks like. With God's grace, we can be brave, even when others around us don't believe in Jesus.

- **Forgive those who hurt us.**

    When someone hurts us, we can show grace by forgiving them, just like God forgives us. We love others because God loved us first (1 John 4:19).

God gives us His grace because He loves us, not because we deserve it. We can't earn it or repay Him. Through His grace, God **forgives** our sins, makes us **His children**, and gives us the **power** to live in this broken world.

Let's share God's amazing grace with others!

3-2 Amazing Grace

Truth to Remember

I am saved by God's grace, not by my works. God's grace is enough for me.

My grace is sufficient for you,
for my power is made perfect in weakness…..

2 Corinthians 12:9 (NIV)

FACT CHECK

GRACE MAKES CHRISTIANITY UNIQUE

Questions: Have you ever wondered what makes Christianity different from other religions?

Answer: Christianity is the only religion that has the concept of **grace.**

Dr. Craig J. Hazen (a Professor of Comparative Religion and Christian Apologetics at Biola University) explains that other religions might talk about mercy and compassion, but Christianity is the only one with grace. God doesn't just say, "I won't punish you for what you did." He goes **above and beyond** by giving us an **amazing gift**: complete forgiveness and eternal life!

Dr. Hazen shares a story from the Bible about a son who made a lot of mistakes and decided to go back home. Instead of being upset, his dad forgave him and threw a huge party to celebrate his return (Luke 15:11–32). In other religions, someone like the son might have to work really hard to fix what they did wrong before being accepted again.[1]

This shows how special God's grace is. He forgives us completely, welcomes us into His family, and gives us eternal life—all because He loves us. Isn't that amazing?

THE SCIENCE BEHIND THE "PEPPER LIFTING" EXPERIMENT

Did you know there's something called **static electricity** that makes the pepper jump to the spoon? Let's learn how it works!

Have you ever walked on a carpet and felt a tiny shock when you touched something metal? Or gone down a slide and zapped your friend with a little spark? That's static electricity in action!

So, what makes static electricity happen? Everything around us, including spoons and cloth, is made of tiny building blocks called **atoms**. Atoms have even smaller parts inside them: **protons** (positive charge,+) and **electrons** (negative charge,-).

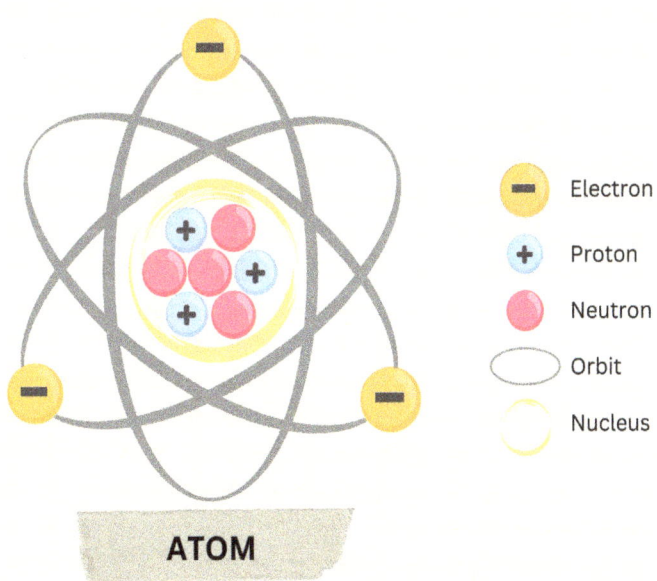

3-2 Amazing Grace

Static electricity happens when electrons (-) move from one object to another. For example, when you rub a spoon with a cloth, some electrons jump from the cloth to the spoon. This makes the spoon **negatively charged**.

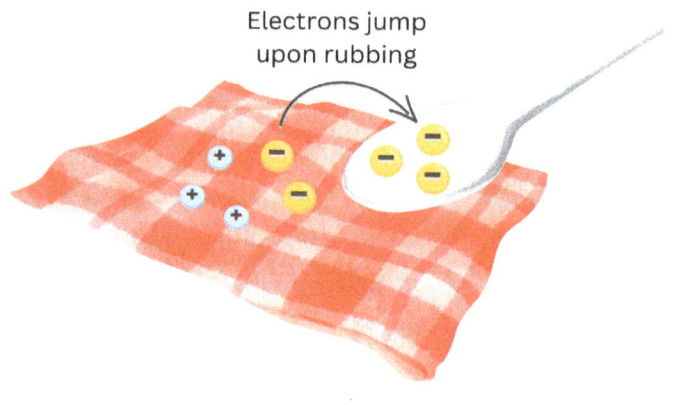

Electrons jump upon rubbing

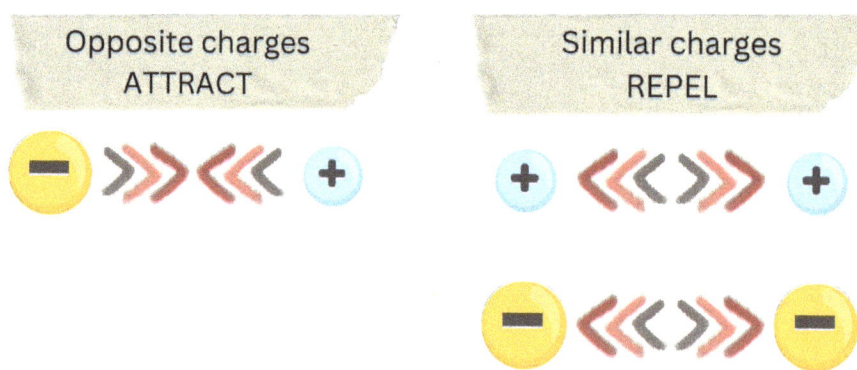

Opposite charges ATTRACT

Similar charges REPEL

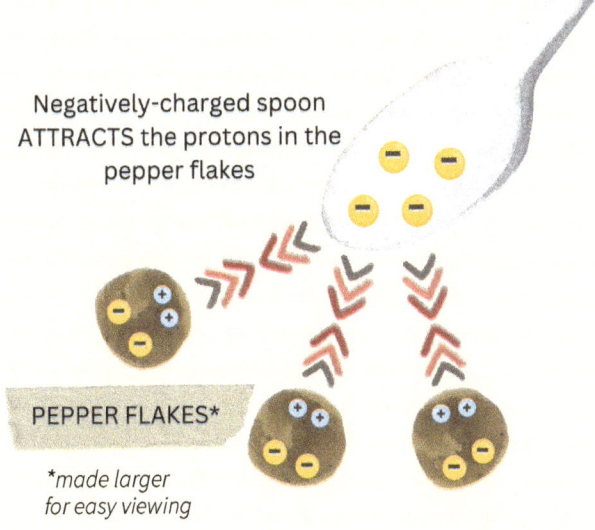

Now, when you bring the negatively charged spoon close to the pepper, the pepper (which has a positive charge) gets pulled toward the spoon—just like how magnets stick together! Pepper is very light, so it jumps to the spoon. Salt is heavier, so it doesn't stick as easily.

Static electricity is so cool, isn't it?

NOTE: Before the next lesson, test yeast for freshness if you have it at home. Purchase new yeast if necessary.

3-3

Jesus Christ: Fact or Fiction?

3-3 Jesus Christ: Fact or Fiction?

NOTE: *Test the freshness of the yeast before the lesson if it has been stored at home for some time.*

PURPOSE

To establish that Jesus Christ is a real historical figure and not merely a spiritual or mythical character created by Christians.

Icebreaker

- If you could meet anyone from the Bible, who would it be and why? What would you ask or say to him or her? *(Parents may share their answers too.)*
- Let's play a quick **Bible Trivia game**!

    How many books are there in the Bible?

    (**Answer**: 66 books)

    ▶ The Bible is split into two main parts. What are they?

    (**Answer**: the Old Testament and the New Testament)

    ▶ The New Testament starts with the birth of Jesus. What do we call the first four books that tell the story of Jesus' life?

    (**Answer**: The first four books in the New Testament are called the "gospels," which means "Good News."[1])

    ▶ What are the names of the four gospels?

    (**Answer**: The four gospels are: Matthew, Mark, Luke, and John.)

3-3 *Jesus Christ: Fact or Fiction?*

Long ago, when Adam and Eve first sinned, God promised to send a special Savior to help us (Genesis 3:15). This promised deliverer is also called the "Messiah."

But He didn't come right away! It took a very long time—about 4,000 years! During that time, many things happened, and those stories are recorded in the Old Testament.

In the Old Testament, God gave people rules or "**the Law**" to follow, but they struggled to keep them. They failed so many times! They needed a Savior because they couldn't do it on their own. The Old Testament also has special messages called **prophecies*** that talk about the Savior who would come in the future.

Then, in the New Testament, we finally meet the promised Savior—Jesus! The first four books, called the **gospels**, tell all about Him: how He was born, what He did, how He died and came back to life. The rest of the New Testament shows us how to follow Jesus.

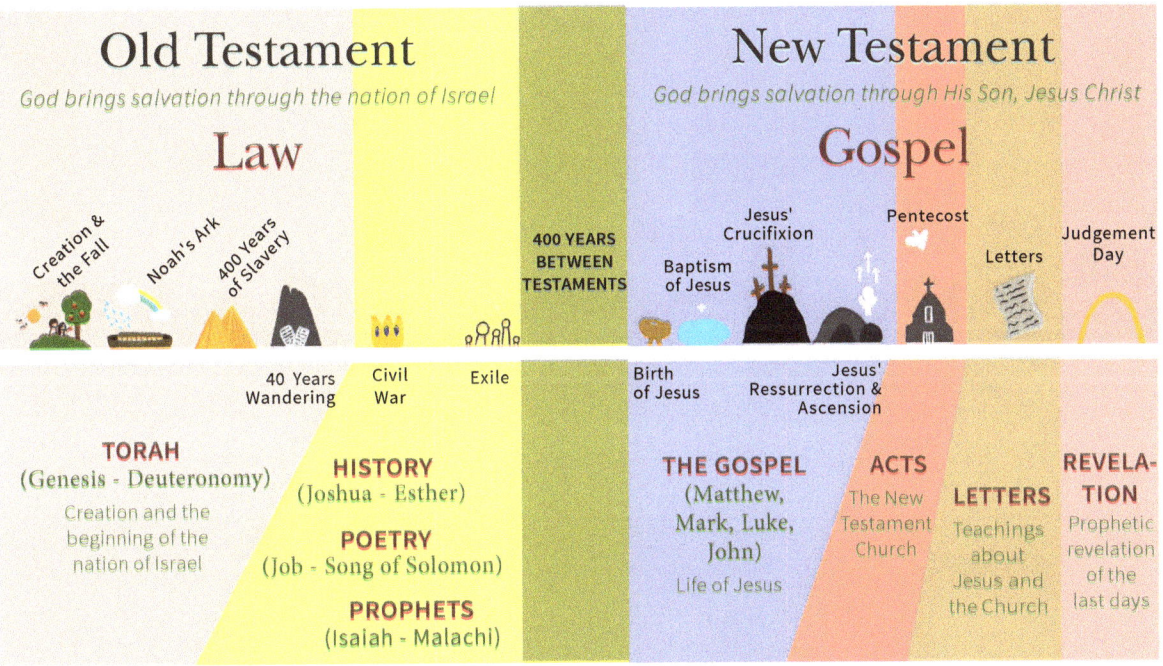

So, the whole Bible tells us about Jesus, the amazing Savior who came to help us. Now, here's a big question:

Is Jesus real, or is He just a made-up character?

***Prophecy** *is a special message or prediction about something that will happen in the future.*

NON-BIBLICAL VIEW

Many people wonder if Jesus really existed. In fact, a survey in England found that nearly half of the teens there don't believe Jesus was a real person who lived on Earth.[2]

Some people, called atheists, don't believe in God. They think that Christians, who already believe in Jesus, wrote the Bible and maybe made up the story about Him.

But is there evidence outside the Bible? Is there proof that Jesus was a real person?

BIBLICAL VIEW

The New Testament shows us that Jesus made **many Old Testament prophecies** about the coming Savior **come true**. If only one or two of them come true, we might think, "Oh, that was just a lucky guess!" But do you know how many Old Testament prophecies about Jesus came true?

> ## Over 300 prophecies from different people, at different times, came true in Jesus' life.

That's a lot, right? It's not just pure luck! *(Check the list of fulfilled prophecies in the **Fact Check** section.)*

John 12:16 (CEV) says:

> *At first, Jesus' disciples did not understand. But after he had been given his glory, they remembered all this.* **Everything had happened exactly as the Scriptures said it would.**

To prove Jesus is real, we also need to look for **proof** *outside* the Bible. And guess what? There *is* proof! Many people who didn't believe in Jesus wrote about Him. Scientists have also found things that show Jesus really lived on Earth over 2,000 years ago. (We will talk about this proof later.)

Today, we're going to explore some invisible things—things we can't see with our eyes. Let's see how they can help us understand more about Jesus.

Activity

The Invisible Force

MATERIALS

- A balloon
- One packet or 2 ¼ teaspoons dry yeast
- One teaspoon sugar
- One cup of warm water *(Make sure it is not too hot.)*
- A bowl
- A funnel or a measuring cup
- A bottle

Note:
Using fresh yeast is crucial for this experiment. If you're unsure about the freshness of your yeast, test it by following these steps:

1. Fill a cup halfway with warm water.
2. Stir in one teaspoon of sugar.
3. Add one packet or 2 ¼ teaspoons of yeast to the sugar water.
4. Place the cup in a warm area and let it sit for 10 minutes undisturbed. The mixture should foam and expand to nearly double its original volume.
5. If this doesn't happen, the yeast may no longer be active. Discard it and use fresh yeast.

BEFORE THE ACTIVITY:

Open the packet of dry yeast (or measure 2 ¼ teaspoons of dry yeast) and pour it into a small bowl. Keep it hidden from the children until it's time to use it.

3-3 Jesus Christ: Fact or Fiction?

INSTRUCTIONS

1. Show the bowl of dry yeast to the children and ask:

   "Do you know what this is?"

   "Is it a living or non-living thing? What made you think so?"

   "We'll find out soon if your answer is right!"

2. Mix dry yeast, one teaspoon of sugar, and one cup of warm water in a bowl.

3. Use a funnel or measuring cup to pour the mixture into a bottle.

4. Ask children:

   "What do you think will happen to the balloon if we stretch it over the bottleneck?"

5. Stretch the balloon over the bottleneck and put it in a warm spot for **about 15-20 minutes.** (Yeast needs a warm, moist environment to be active.) Watch what happens as the yeast starts working.

Note:
This experiment requires some waiting, so remind the children that sometimes great things take time and don't always happen instantly.

While waiting, you can:

- *Explore the **Fact Check** section, learning about evidence supporting Jesus' existence and the calendar system.*

- *For **younger** children: Discuss three prophecies about Jesus from **Fact #1**, read the Bible verses, and show pictures from **Fact #4** that provide historical evidence of Jesus' life and ministry.*

- *Engage the children by asking questions about the objects shown in the pictures and why they are important in proving Jesus' existence.*

6. Once the balloon is inflated, continue to the discussion section.

3-3 Jesus Christ: Fact or Fiction?

Discussion

1. Did you guess right about what would happen with the balloon?

2. How would you describe what happened to the balloon?

   *(**Answer:** Yeast is a **living thing**, just like plants and animals. It needs food to stay alive, just like we do! In our experiment, the yeast eats the sugar in the water and makes two things: carbon dioxide gas and a tiny bit of alcohol.*

   Now, here's the cool part: the carbon dioxide gas floats into the bottle and fills up the balloon because it has nowhere else to go! As the yeast keeps eating the sugar, it keeps making more gas, and the balloon fills up even more. The gas gets trapped inside, making the balloon puff up like a balloon you blow up with your breath!)

   *(To learn more about yeast, check out the **Fact Check** section.)*

3. It's tricky to describe things we can't see, like the tiny yeast cells and carbon dioxide gas they made. How did the experiment help you understand that invisible things can be real?

3-3 Jesus Christ: Fact or Fiction?

_____

_____

*(**Answer:** Although we can't see the gas, **we can see what it does**. The gas inflates the balloon. And even though the yeast cells are too tiny to see, we know they're alive because of what they do. They work hard to eat the sugar and make gas.)*

Can *dead* yeast do the same thing? Nope! If we use dead yeast to bake bread, it won't turn out fluffy and soft like we want. Instead, it'll be hard and tough.

So, when we see how yeast works and learn that it's alive, we understand that even though we can't see it, it's still real. Remember, **just because something is invisible doesn't mean it's not there!**

4   Do you find it hard to believe in a God you can't see? Why or why not?

_____

_____

_____

_____

It's true that we can't see God with our eyes. Even when Jesus, God's Son, came to Earth, not everyone believed in Him. One of Jesus' disciple, **Thomas**, had a hard time believing that Jesus was alive again after He died. Jesus told him,

> "You believe because you have seen me.
> Blessed are those who believe without seeing me."
> (John 20:29)

Even though we can't see Jesus the way people did back then, **His work and power are still real today**! When we trust in God, even without seeing Him, we are **blessed**—because our faith is in something real, even if we can't see it!

3-3 Jesus Christ: Fact or Fiction?

5. How would you tell your friends why you believe in Jesus, even though you can't see him now?

   _____

   _____

   _____

   _____

Some of our friends and family might not believe Jesus is real because they can't see Him. But we can show them proof from the Bible and other stories. We can also share how Jesus has changed our lives and helped us every day. The way we act—by showing love, kindness, and helping others—can show them that Jesus is real.

(Parents might want to share their personal stories too: **"What made you decide to follow Jesus?"***)*

If you want to learn more about whether Jesus is real, check out the **Fact Check** section. There are lots of writings from Christian, Jewish, and Roman people that show Jesus really lived on Earth.

— Summary —

How do we know Jesus is real?

- Many **prophecies** written in the Bible about Jesus long before He was born really **came true**.
- People who saw Jesus when He was alive **told** others about Him. Even experts who weren't Christians **wrote** about Him.
- Scientists have also found **things and places** that show Jesus really lived on Earth.

Even though we can't see Jesus like we see our friends, it doesn't mean He's not real. His love and power still change lives today!

Truth to Remember

Jesus Christ is real. He was a part of history, and I want Him to be a part of my story too.

Then Jesus told him,
"You believe because you have seen me.
Blessed are those who believe without seeing me."

John 20:29

3-3 Jesus Christ: Fact or Fiction?

FACT CHECK

IS JESUS REAL ?

Fact #1: Over 300 prophecies about the coming Messiah/ Savior in the Old Testament came true in Jesus' life.

These prophecies were made **hundreds of years before** Jesus was born, and they came true in amazing ways!

If you want to see for yourself, you can read these special stories in the Old Testament and see how they match with what happened in Jesus' life:

- **Zechariah 11-13** (written about 500 years before Jesus)
- **Isaiah 53** (written about 700 years before Jesus)
- **Psalm 22** (written by King David about 1000 years before Jesus)

Here are some examples of prophecies about Jesus:

Prophecies about Jesus	Prophecy (Old Testament)	When it Happened (New Testament)
The Messiah would be born of a virgin.	Isaiah 7:14	Matthew 1:22-23 Luke 1:26-31
The Messiah would be born in Bethlehem.	Micah 5:2	Matthew 2:1 Luke 2:4-6
The Messiah would come from the tribe of Judah.	Genesis 49:10	Luke 3:33 Hebrews 7:14
The Messiah would be rejected by His own people.	Psalm 69:8 Isaiah 53:3	John 1:11 John 7:5

Prophecies about Jesus	**Prophecy (Old Testament)**	**When it Happened (New Testament)**
The Messiah would be betrayed and "sold" for 30 pieces of silver.	Psalm 41:9 Zechariah 11:12–13	Luke 22:47–48 Matthew 26:14–16
The Messiah's hands and feet would be pierced.	Psalm 22:16 Zechariah 12:10	John 20:25–27
Soldiers would pierce the Messiah's side.	Zechariah 12:10	John 19:34
The Messiah's bones would not be broken.	Exodus 12:46 Psalm 34:20	John 19:33–36
The Messiah would rise again from the dead.	Psalm 16:10 Psalm 49:15	Matthew 28:2–7 Acts 2:22–32
The Messiah would go up to heaven.	Psalm 24:7–10	Mark 16:19 Luke 24:51

More examples of prophecies are in the **Notes** section if you want to learn more.[3,4]

Fact #2: There are books in the Bible written by people who knew Jesus or heard about Him from other eyewitnesses.

The New Testament books were written when many people who saw Jesus were still alive. These books tell us true stories about Jesus and also describe how people lived during that time, especially the Jewish people.[5]

1. **Paul** wrote many letters, called **epistles**, to different churches and people between A.D. 48 and 60. Out of the 21 epistles in the New Testament, he wrote at least 13 of them.

2. The four **gospels**, which provide detailed biographies of Jesus, were written within the first century by:

    - **Mark** (around A.D. 60)
    - **Matthew** and **Luke** (around A.D. 60-70)
    - **John** (around A.D. 90-100)

Fact #3: Non-Christian writers mentioned Jesus *outside* the Bible.

Many years after Jesus lived on Earth, **Jewish and Roman historians** who were **not** His followers mentioned Him in their writings. Since they didn't believe in Jesus, what they wrote is important because it helps prove that the things we read about Jesus in the Bible are true.[6]

Flavius Josephus

- A Jewish historian and military leader
- Famous work: *The Antiquities of the Jews* (a 20-volume book series about history of the Jewish people written in A.D. 93-94)
- In one passage of *Antiquities of the Jew*, Josephus describes Jesus:

"Now there was about this time **Jesus, a wise man**, if it be lawful to call him a man; for he was a **doer of wonderful works, a teacher** of such men as receive the truth with pleasure. He drew over to him both many of the Jews and many of the Gentiles.

He was [the] Christ. And when **Pilate**, at the suggestion of the principal men amongst us, **had condemned him to the cross**, those that loved him at the first did not forsake him; for he appeared to them **alive again the third day**; as the divine prophets had foretold these and ten thousand other wonderful things concerning him." *(book XVIII chapter 3, emphasis added)*[7]

Tacitus

- A Roman senator and historian
- Famous work: *Annals of Imperial Rome* (a first-century history of the Roman Empire written in around A.D. 116)
- When telling the story of the burning of Rome in A.D. 64, Tacitus mentioned Roman Emperor Nero falsely blaming "the persons commonly called Christians, who were hated for their enormities. **Christus, the founder of the name, was put to death by Pontius Pilate, procurator of Judea in the reign of Tiberius.**"

(*Christus* = Christ in Latin)

Pliny the Younger

- A Roman governor
- Pliny wrote a letter to Roman Emperor Trajan around A.D. 112 and asked for counsel on dealing with early Christians. He mentioned **early Christians would "sing hymns to Christ as to a god."**

Fact #4: Archaeological findings.[8]

- On the **Sea of Galilee**, where Jesus spent a lot of His time teaching and doing miracles, archaeologists made an amazing discovery: **a Galilean fishing boat from the time of Jesus**! It was found during a drought, and it's just like the boats that Jesus' disciples would have used.

    This shows us something real from the time when Jesus lived!

A first-century Galilean fishing boat:
Jesus and His disciple might have used this type of boat on the Sea of Galilee.

3-3 Jesus Christ: Fact or Fiction?

- In **Capernaum**, a town Jesus often visited, there's a special place called the "**White Synagogue**." It was built a long time ago, in the late fourth century A.D., on top of an even **older synagogue from the time of Jesus**. Jesus did incredible things there, like healing a man with an evil spirit (Luke 4:31-37) and teaching about the bread of life (John 6:25-59).

  This shows us a real place where Jesus once taught and performed miracles!

White Synagogue: Jesus used to teach in a synagogue or a place of worship previously built here.

- Also in **Capernaum**, the **house where Peter lived** is still there today, although a Christian church was built over it in the fifth century A.D.[9]

  This site is a special place for many, as it is believed to be where Jesus performed miracles, including healing Peter's mother-in-law (Mark 1:29-31).

House of Peter in Capernaum:
Jesus once came into Peter's house to heal his sick mother-in-law.

(For more archaeological findings, check out the **Notes** section.)

DID YOU KNOW WHAT B.C. AND A.D. MEAN?

The terms "B.C." and "A.D." are used to label or number years in the Julian and Gregorian calendars, with Jesus Christ as the central focus.

"B.C." means **"Before Christ,"** referring to the time before Jesus was born.

"A.D." stands for the Latin phrase **Anno Domini**, which means **"in the year of our Lord."**

There is no year zero in this system, so the year A.D. 1 (when Jesus was born) immediately follows the year 1 B.C.

THE SCIENCE BEHIND "THE INVISIBLE FORCE" EXPERIMENT

Yeast is a tiny single-celled fungus, and there are about 160 different species of yeast. Even though yeast cells are so small and you can't see them with your eyes, there are millions of them in just one small granule of dry yeast!

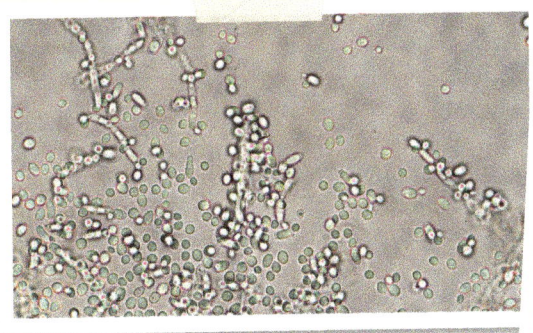

Baker's yeast (Saccharomyces cerevisiae) *under the microscope.*

Yeast has been helping bread rise for thousands of years. But how does it work? Well, yeast loves to eat sugars and starches. When it eats these sugars, it breaks them down to get energy, just like we do when we eat food. But here's the cool part: when yeast eats sugar, it creates two things as waste—carbon dioxide gas and ethanol. This process is called "**fermentation**."

Now, you might be wondering how this helps bread. The carbon dioxide gas that yeast creates during fermentation is what makes bread rise and become fluffy. Those little holes you see in bread? That's from the carbon dioxide gas getting trapped in the dough and causing it to expand. So, next time you see enjoy some soft, fluffy bread, you can thank the yeast for helping it rise!

NOTE: In the next lesson, we'll be making ice cream. Since some kids might be excited to taste their creations right away, be sure to plan your time accordingly.

3-4

Jesus Christ:
Fully God, Fully Man

3-4 Jesus Christ: Fully God, Fully Man

NOTE: *This activity involves making a dessert together. Plan ahead to determine when you want to do the lesson. You may allow them to enjoy their dessert while going through the discussion questions.*

PURPOSE

To explore the evidence of Jesus' humanity and understand why it is crucial.

Icebreaker

- If you could go anywhere in the world, where would you want to visit and what would you do there?

- Would you rather visit your dream place **in person** or take a **virtual tour** from home? Why would you choose that?

In our last lesson, we learned that Jesus isn't just a character in a story—He's real! Today, we're continuing our journey to learn more about Jesus, the most important person in history.

When we think of superheroes, we imagine them flying in from the sky or making a big, dramatic entrance. But Jesus did something totally unexpected! He came into the world as a tiny, helpless baby, born in a simple manger, not a grand palace!

This is so different from what people expected a Savior to be like. So, let's think about a big question:

Is Jesus God, or was He just a man?

. . .

NON-BIBLICAL VIEW

Many people during Jesus' time (and even today) had a hard time believing that Jesus was God. Some thought He was just *a man* pretending to be God. They even accused Him of disrespecting God's name. Because of this, Jesus was punished and put to death on a cross.

Since we can't see Jesus face-to-face, it might be hard to picture Him as a real person. Even in the early church, some people spread lies, saying Jesus wasn't really human (2 John 1:7).

Sometimes, we might feel the same way. Since we can't see Jesus, we might wonder if He really understands what it's like to be us. We might even think that God is far away and doesn't know how we feel. But here's an important question:

Does Jesus understand when we are sad or having a hard time?

 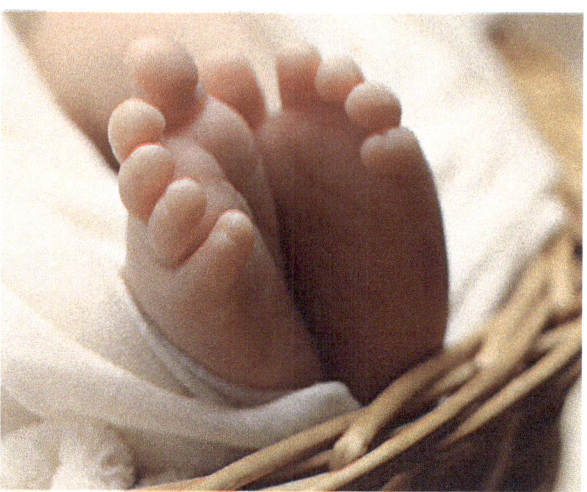

BIBLICAL VIEW

Let's dive into what the Bible says about who Jesus really is.

Jesus is unique because He is both **fully God** and **fully human** at the same time when He lived on Earth.

That's a big thing to understand, but let's break it down!

First, Jesus said that **He is God** (John 8:58). He **did things that only God can do**, like forgiving sins and performing amazing miracles. But at the same time, Jesus **lived just like any other human**. He had a body, feelings, and thoughts just like we do. He could sweat when He was scared, feel hungry after fasting for 40 days, and go through all sorts of emotions like being tired, angry, sad, or happy.

Even though Jesus is God, He chose to live a simple, humble life. He didn't live in a grand palace or wear fancy clothes. Instead, He worked as a carpenter before He started His ministry. Jesus was born as a tiny baby and even died on the cross to show His love and sacrifice for us (Philippians 2:6-8). Isn't it amazing that Jesus, who is both God and man, chose to live this way for us?

So why did an amazing God choose to become human like us?

Hebrews 2:14 says:

> Because God's children are human beings—made of flesh and blood—the Son also became flesh and blood. For **only as a human being could he die**, and only **by dying could he break the power of the devil**, who had the power of death.

Jesus had to become fully human so He could **die for our sins** and **set us free** (Hebrews 2:17). But there's even more good news: Because Jesus faced suffering and testing just like us, He can **help us when we face challenges** too (Hebrews 2:18).

Jesus knows exactly what it's like to be human. He understands our feelings and experiences because He went through them Himself!

Now, let's use our five senses (sight, smell, hearing, touch, and taste) just like Jesus did when He walked on Earth. Today, we're making a delicious treat together: ice cream! With just five simple ingredients, we'll create something yummy. Are you ready for a sensory adventure? Let's get started!

Activity

Homemade Ice Cream-In-a-Bag

MATERIALS

The following measurement is for one serving of ice cream. You can increase the amounts to make more servings as needed.

- 1/2 cup half-and-half, heavy cream, or non-dairy milk alternatives
- 1 tablespoon sugar
- 1/4 teaspoon vanilla for flavor *(or other flavors)*
- 3 cups ice
- 1/3 cup salt *(rock salt or regular table salt)*
- Gallon-size sealable plastic zip-style bag(s)
- Quart-size sealable plastic zip-style bag(s)
- Kitchen towel/potholder *(to handle the cold bag)*
- Cold tap water *(for rinsing)*
- A small ice cream bowl
- Optional toppings and mix-ins: sprinkles, chocolate sauce, fruits, crushed Oreo cookies, mini marshmallows
- A music player *(optional—to add more fun during the ice cream shaking time)*

Flavor Ideas

- 2 strawberries (chopped) — STRAWBERRY
- 1 teaspoon cacao powder — CHOCOLATE
- 5 drops peppermint extract, 2 teaspoons chocolate chips — MINT CHOCOLATE CHIP
- 1 teaspoon cacao powder, mini marshmallows — ROCKY ROAD
- 3 Oreo cookies (crushed) — COOKIES & CREAM

Tips to prevent salt from leaking into the ice cream mixture:

- Use high-quality zip-style bags. No-name brands may not provide a good seal, increasing the risk of leaks. If the bag doesn't seal well, double-bag the ice cream mixture for extra protection.

- Both rock salt and regular table salt will work, but rock salt is chunkier and less likely to mix into the ice cream when opening the bag.

INSTRUCTIONS

1. Decide which ice cream flavors you'd like to make.

2. Add half-and-half, sugar, and vanilla extract (or your chosen flavoring) to a quart-sized bag and seal tightly. You can add toppings and mix-ins (such as fruits, cookies, and chocolate chips) *after* the ice cream has formed.

   Tip: Double-bag the quart-sized bag to prevent leaking.

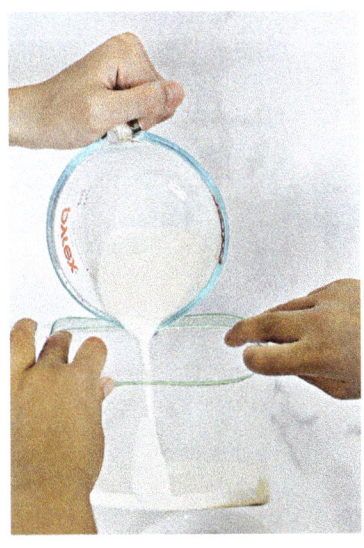

3. Add ice and salt into a gallon-sized bag.

4. Place the quart-sized bag containing the ice cream mixture inside the gallon bag with ice and salt. Seal both bags tightly.

5. Double-check to ensure that both bags are well-sealed to prevent leaks.

6. Shake the bags vigorously or gently knead them for 5-10 minutes, until the ice cream mixture becomes thick and creamy.

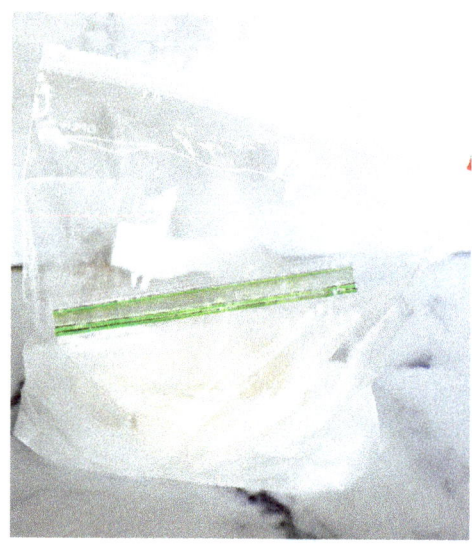

Tips:

- **Make it fun:** *Play music, have a dance party, jump around while shaking, or toss the bags back and forth—but be careful not to drop them!*
- **Protect your hands:** *Use towels or potholders to hold the bags, as they can get very cold.*

7. Once the ice cream forms, remove the smaller bag containing the ice cream and rinse its top (above the seal) with cold water to wash away any salt.

8. Open the ice cream bag carefully to ensure no salt gets into your tasty ice cream treat.

9. Scoop the ice cream into a small bowl and add your favorite toppings or mix-ins.

10. Enjoy your homemade treat while you dive into the discussion!

   Note: If your ice cream is softer than you'd like, place it in the freezer for 15-20 minutes to firm it up before serving.

Discussion

1. Let's talk about our five senses. Can you name them? How did you use your five senses while making ice cream today?

   (Answer: We saw the ice cream ingredients, smelled the yummy vanilla, felt the cold ice, heard the fun music while shaking, and tasted how delicious the ice cream is.)

   *(For the science behind the experiment, check out the **Fact Check** section.)*

2. Did you know Jesus experienced these five senses too while He lived on Earth? This shows that Jesus was **fully human**! Can you think of some things He saw, heard, tasted, smelled, and touched during His time on Earth?

   (Answer: For example, Jesus saw the blind man, touched the lepers, smelled Lazarus's body after he died, heard the waves and the wind, tasted the bread and fish, and many other examples.)

   *(Find more evidence of Jesus' humanity in the **Fact Check** section.)*

3. When Jesus was on Earth, He faced **challenges** just like we do. Can you think of some things that Jesus went through that we also experience?

3-4 Jesus Christ: Fully God, Fully Man

(Answer:

- *Jesus was **tempted** just like we are.*
- *Jesus **learned to obey** His parents on Earth and His Father in heaven.*
- *Jesus **understands how it feels** to be doubted, rejected, embarrassed, betrayed, and even left alone by His closest friends.)*

4. How was Jesus different from a "regular" person?

   _____

   _____

   (Answer: *Jesus was tempted, but He **did not sin**.)*

   Hebrews 4:15 says,

   > "This High Priest of ours **understands our weaknesses**, for he faced all of the same testings we do, yet **he did not sin.**"

   So, when we feel like we want to do something wrong, Jesus can help us choose the right thing instead.

5. Jesus became fully human and understands how we feel and think. How do you feel knowing that Jesus truly understands you?

   _____

   _____

Summary

Remember, God isn't far away. He walked in our shoes before, so **He understands our struggles and cares for us**. We can talk to Him anytime we need help. Our loving God is always ready to help us in everything we do!

3-4 Jesus Christ: Fully God, Fully Man

Truth to Remember

Lord Jesus became fully human to save us completely.

He truly is a wonderful Savior!

This High Priest of ours understands our weaknesses, for he faced all of the same testings we do, yet he did not sin.

Hebrews 4:15

FACT CHECK

THE SCIENCE BEHIND THE "ICE-CREAM-IN-A-BAG"

Have you ever seen salt on sidewalks during winter? It's there to help melt ice. We're using the same idea to make homemade ice cream!

When we put ice and salt in a bag, the salt helps the ice melt, but it also makes the ice get even colder. This super cold ice helps freeze the ice cream mix. As the mix gets colder, it turns into yummy ice cream. It's a fun and easy way to make a cool treat at home!

EVIDENCE FOR JESUS' HUMANITY ON EARTH

Jesus had a **human body, heart, emotions, mind, and will**. The Bible is clear about these aspects of His humanity. Let's explore some evidence from the Bible that shows Jesus was truly human while He was on Earth.

(You can refer to this list as you read the Gospels. Take your time and don't feel like you need to go through everything all at once.)

Jesus had a human BODY	
He was born from a woman.	Matthew 1:25, Luke 2:7
He grew tired and sat by the well in Samaria.	John 4:6
He slept in the boat during the storm.	Matthew 8:24, Mark 4:38, Luke 8:23
He became hungry.	Matthew 4:2, Mark 11:12, Luke 4:2
He became thirsty.	John 19:28
He died and shed blood.	Luke 23:46, John 19:34
After His resurrection, He had a real human body.	Luke 24:39–43, John 20:20, 27

Jesus had a human HEART and EMOTIONS	
He got angry when He saw people buying and selling in the temple.	Matthew 21:12–13, Mark 11:15, John 2:15–17
He was sad and mourned. He cried: • when He saw those He loved, Mary and Martha, crying over the death of their brother Lazarus;	John 11:33–35
• when He prayed in the Garden of Gethsemane before His death on the cross.	Hebrews 5:7, Matthew 26:38
He felt a strong desire to help others.	Matthew 14:14, 15:32

Jesus had a human MIND	
Jesus "grew in wisdom." This means He wasn't born knowing everything. Instead, He learned and grew over time, just like we do.	Luke 2:52

Jesus had human WILL	
He chose to obey his parents on Earth: "Then he returned to Nazareth with them and was *obedient* to them…"	Luke 2:51
He chose to obey his heavenly Father: "For I have come down from heaven to do the will of God who sent me, not to do my own will."	John 6:38
Jesus prayed to the Father, "Yet I want your will to be done, not mine."	Matthew 26:39

NOTE: For the next lesson, we recommend parents try the activity beforehand to find the best plate and glass combination

3-5

The Cross: Fact or Fiction?

3-5 The Cross: Fact or Fiction?

NOTE: *Try the activity beforehand to find which plate and glass combination works best.*

PURPOSE

To understand the significance of the cross as a universal Christian symbol.

Icebreaker

- Can you think of symbols or signs you see a lot?
- What is a symbol that Christians use? Where do you usually see it?

  (**Answer**: *The cross. You might see it on Bible covers, church buildings, bumper stickers, jewelry, clothing, and more.*)

3-5 The Cross: Fact or Fiction?

Have you ever wondered:

Why Christian use the cross as a symbol?

A long time ago, the cross was a very scary symbol. It was a way that people were punished, and it was painful. Even the toughest people didn't want to die on a cross!

So why would Christians choose a symbol like that? It might seem strange, but there's a special reason behind it.

. . .

NON-BIBLICAL VIEW

Did you know that today, even people who aren't Christians sometimes wear a cross? Some wear it as jewelry, or just because they think it looks cool. But do you think they know what it *really* means?

We've all heard the story about how Jesus died on the cross, but some people don't believe it's true! They wonder, **"Is there any proof it really happened?"** And **if God is so powerful, why would He let Jesus die in such a sad and painful way on a cross?** It seems like such a terrible way to go, doesn't it?

BIBLICAL VIEW

First, why do you think Jesus had to die? Remember that **everyone has sinned**, and the punishment is **eternal death** (Romans 6:23). That means being separated from God forever. And everyone—including you and me—has to pay this price!

Because God is holy and perfect, sin separates us from Him.

So how can we, who are sinful, become friends with a perfect God?

Well, in Old Testament times, people had to bring a **perfect, spotless animal** to be sacrificed when they made a mistake. They had to do this *over* and *over* to make peace with God. Can you imagine if we still had to do that today? It would be like bringing a big cow or goat to church every time we did something wrong! That would be so hard—and really messy!

As part of God's amazing plan to save us from the punishment of death, He provided the perfect sacrifice **once and for all**: His own Son, Jesus Christ. **John 3:16** (NIV) says:

> *For God so loved the world that he gave his one and only Son, that whoever believes in him shall not perish but have eternal life.*

Jesus is the only perfect "Lamb of God" because He is spotless—He never sinned.

We can't save ourselves, so Jesus took our punishment by dying on the cross.

Even today, Jesus' death on the cross is one of the most important moments in history. He was treated terribly—given a crown of thorns, beaten, mocked, and hung on the cross. But He never gave up. He chose to die to save us **because He loves us so much**.

Now, let's do an activity to help us understand what happened at the cross.

3-5 The Cross: Fact or Fiction?

Activity
Disappearing Sin

MATERIALS

- A glass plate with a smooth, flat bottom

- A clear drinking glass or jar

- A penny (or any other coin)

- A votive or tea light candle that fits inside the glass or jar

- Lighter or matches

- A cup of water

- Food coloring

Note: *Different plates and glasses can change how much water is drawn into the glass. Pick the plate and glass combination that draws the most water for the best effect.*

89

3-5 The Cross: Fact or Fiction?

INSTRUCTIONS

1. Show the kids a penny and ask:

    "Whose picture is on this penny?"

    *"Since this penny has a picture of a person, let's imagine it's **us**."*

2. Place the penny slightly off-center on the plate.
3. Take a cup of water and add a drop of food coloring to it. Stir it well and say:

    *"This colored water is like **our sins**."*

4. Pour just enough colored water over the penny to barely cover the coin. You might only need a few tablespoons. Say:

   *"Romans 3:23 tells us that **everyone has sinned** and falls short of God's glory. That means **all** of us have sinned, except for Jesus."*

5. Show the candle to the kids and say:

   *"This candle represents **Jesus**. He said in John 8:12 that **He is the light of the world**. Whoever follows Him will never walk in darkness, but will have the light of life."*

6. Place the candle in the middle of the plate, light it, and say:

   *"The Bible tells us that Jesus came to Earth to pay the price of our sins. The flame is like **Jesus' life**, shining as the light of the world."*

7. Hold the glass up and say:

   *"This glass is like **the cross**. When the glass covers the candle, it's like Jesus being hung on the cross."*

   "Now watch carefully as we cover the candle."

8. Place the glass over the candle and observe what happens.

   *(As soon as the glass is placed flat on the plate, the colored water will start moving into the glass. When the candle goes out—symbolizing **Jesus' death**—the rest of the water will be drawn into the glass.)*

   Note:
   Some water might stay on the plate, and we'll talk about that during the discussion.

9. After the water stops moving into the glass, say:

   "When Jesus died on the cross, He took our sins away, just like 1 Peter 2:24 says: 'He personally carried our sins in his body on the cross so that we can be dead to sin and live for what is right.'"

   *"The candle went out just like **Jesus died to take away our sins**."*

3-5 The Cross: Fact or Fiction?

1. Do you remember what happened to the candle when we covered it with the glass? What does it represent?

   (**Answer:** *The flame went out. This represents Jesus' death on the cross.*)

2. What happened to the colored water when the flame went out?

   (**Answer:** *Most of the colored water was drawn into the glass. You can check the* **Fact Check** *section for the science behind it.*)

   Just like the candle drew the water away from the penny, Jesus gave up His life to **take our sins upon Himself** *and set us free. (Pick up the penny and show it to the children.) The penny is no longer covered in sin, and neither are we when we trust Jesus as our Savior!*

3. (**Optional**—if any liquid is left on the penny). Did you see any liquid left on the penny?
   - Temptation and sin are always around us. We still make mistakes and bad choices, even as Christians. That's why we need Jesus every day—every minute of our lives.

3-5 The Cross: Fact or Fiction?

4. On the cross, Jesus cried out in a loud voice, "My God, my God, why have you abandoned me?" (Matthew 27:46 and Mark 15:34). Why do you think Jesus said that? Did God the Father really turn away and leave Jesus?

_____

_____

_____

*(**Answer:** Yes, for a moment, God the Father had to turn away from Jesus. Jesus was perfect and never sinned, but on the cross, He took all the sins of the world on Himself. Since God is completely holy, He cannot be near sin. So when Jesus carried our sins, God had to look away for a short time. But Jesus obeyed His Father and went through this separation so that we could be saved.)*

5. A long time ago, in the temple of God, there was a special room called the **Most Holy Place**. This room was very sacred because it held **the Ark of the Covenant**, which showed that God was there.

   A big **curtain** separated the Most Holy Place from the rest of the temple. It was like a **wall** between God and the people. Only the high priest was allowed to go behind that curtain—and only once a year! He had to offer a special sacrifice to God for the people's sins.

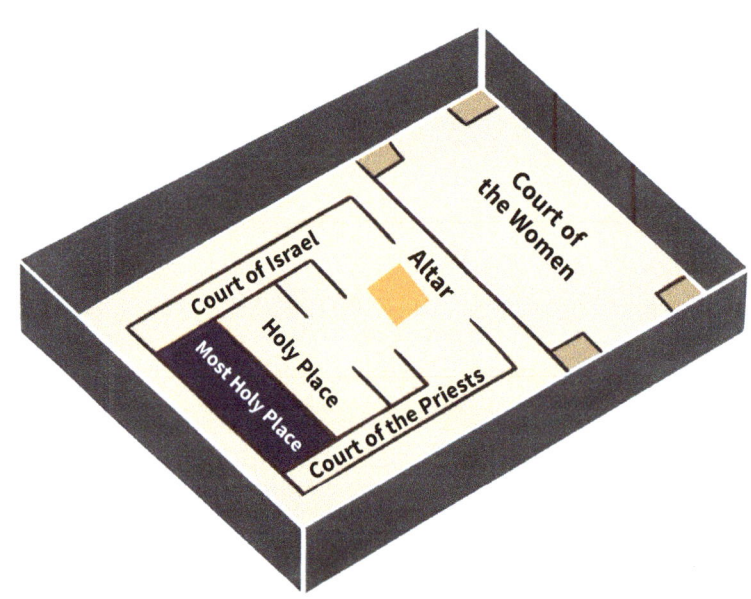

Look at this picture. Can you guess what happened to the curtain? (**Hint**: Read Matthew 27:51)

*(**Answer:** Right after Jesus died on the cross, the curtain in the Temple was torn in two, from top to bottom. The earth shook, and rocks split apart.)*

After the curtain was torn, **nothing separated us from God** anymore. Jesus' sacrifice on the cross made a way for us to be close to God. Now, we can talk directly to Him anytime, anywhere! Isn't that amazing?

6. Read **1 Peter 1:18–19** together.

   *For you know that **God paid a ransom** [payment made to set someone free] to save you from the empty life you inherited from your ancestors. And it was not paid with mere gold or silver, which lose their value. It was the **precious blood of Christ**, the **sinless, spotless Lamb of God**.*

Jesus died on the cross to pay the full price of our sins and set us free from the punishment we deserved. How does that make you feel? Let's take a moment to thank and praise Him from our hearts today!

Summary

The cross isn't just something cool or trendy. It has a very special meaning for those who believe in Jesus. It reminds us of when **Jesus**, God's perfect lamb, **gave His life once and for all** to save us from our sins. He did this because He loves us unconditionally.

Thanks to Jesus, everyone can now be **friends with God**. We can talk to Him directly whenever we want, no matter where we are.

3-5 The Cross: Fact or Fiction?

Truth to Remember

On the cross, Jesus died as a perfect sacrifice to pay for our sins.

He personally carried our sins in his body on the cross
so that we can be dead to sin and live for what is right.
By his wounds you are healed.

1 Peter 2:24

FACT CHECK

SHORT HISTORY OF THE CROSS

About 2,000 years ago, Jesus was put on a cross in Jerusalem (around 33 A.D.). Back then, the Romans were in charge, and they used crosses to punish people for serious crimes like stealing or rebelling. It was a very painful way to die, and only people who weren't Roman citizens were put on crosses, like slaves or criminals.

The cross was meant to punish and shame people. The person would stay on the cross until they died, often from being tired, losing blood, or having trouble breathing. Sometimes, soldiers would break their legs to make the person die faster. But when the soldiers came to Jesus, He was already dead, so they didn't break His legs. Instead, they pierced His side to make sure He had truly died (John 19:33-36).

The Roman Emperor Constantine later stopped using this punishment in the fourth century A.D.[1]

Did the Romans really use crosses?

Yes! People found an **ancient heel bone with an iron nail** in it in a Jerusalem graveyard.[2] This proves that the Romans did use crosses for punishment during Jesus' time.

This historical information helps us understand the kind of death Jesus endured for us.

EVIDENCE FOR JESUS' LAST DAYS AND CRUCIFIXION

The story of Jesus' crucifixion begins at the **Mount of Olives**, where the **Garden of Gethsemane** is located. This is the place where **Jesus prayed** before He was arrested.

Did you know you can still visit the Garden of Gethsemane today? Some of its ancient olive trees are nearly 2,000 years old. They might have even been there when Jesus prayed![3,4]

Garden of Gethsemane

Not far from the Mount of Olives, across the Kidron Valley, is the **Golden Gate**. This is where Jesus **entered Jerusalem before His trial**.

Archaeologists have discovered evidence about the key figures involved in Jesus' trial and crucifixion:

1. The actual **bones** of the Jewish High Priest, **Caiaphas**, are preserved in an ornate bone box, showing he was a real historical figure.

2. A **tablet** mentions the Roman governor, **Pontius Pilate**, who sentenced Jesus to death.[5,6]

In Jerusalem, you can visit **Gabbatha**, the judgment place of Pontius Pilate.

From there, visitors can walk along the **Via Dolorosa**, the path Jesus took while carrying His cross to **Calvary**, the hill outside Jerusalem where He was crucified.

A tablet with Pontius Pilate written on it

Via Dolorosa

3-5 The Cross: Fact or Fiction?

Today, the **Church of the Holy Sepulchre** stands as a powerful reminder of these events. Many scholars believe it marks the exact locations where **Jesus was crucified and buried.**[7]

Church of the Holy Sepulchre

THE SCIENCE BEHIND THE "DISAPPEARING SIN" EXPERIMENT

When the candle is covered with a glass, it uses up the oxygen inside as it burns. Once the oxygen runs out, the flame goes out.

While the flame burns, it heats the air inside the glass, causing the air to expand. You might even notice bubbles escaping as this happens. When the flame goes out, the air cools quickly, lowering the air pressure inside the glass.

Since air moves from areas of higher pressure to lower pressure, **the higher pressure outside the glass pushes the water from the plate into the glass**. The water keeps rising until the air pressure inside and outside the glass becomes equal.

NOTE: For the next lesson's activity, we recommend parents try it beforehand to practice and prepare.

3-6

Jesus' Resurrection: Fact or Fiction?

3-6 Jesus' Resurrection: Fact or Fiction?

NOTE: Before the lesson, we suggest practicing the activity to prepare.

PURPOSE

To investigate the evidence of Jesus' resurrection and understand its significance.

Icebreaker

- What's your favorite thing to do on Easter?
- Are there any special traditions we do together that make Easter extra fun or meaningful for you?

Families celebrate **Easter** in all sorts of ways! Some kids enjoy meeting the Easter bunny, hunting for colorful eggs, and munching on tasty springtime treats. And let's not forget the excitement of finding surprises in Easter baskets—it's like a mini Christmas in the spring! (Okay, maybe not as big as Christmas, but still super fun!)

Here's a fun Easter fact: Did you know jelly beans were first introduced as an Easter treat in the 1930s? Today, Americans eat over 16 million jelly beans during Easter—that's enough to circle the world three times![1]

Easter is a special time loved by many, not just Christians. People of all backgrounds join in the Easter fun! But do you know why we celebrate Easter every year? What's the real meaning behind it?

Well, you're right! Easter is all about celebrating Jesus rising from the dead. That very first Easter was the day Jesus came back to life after dying on the cross.

3-6 Jesus' Resurrection: Fact or Fiction?

The first Easter was a day of victory because Jesus completed His mission on Earth.

• • •

NON-BIBLICAL VIEW

But even today, many people find it hard to believe that Jesus rose from the dead. Why? Because it doesn't seem scientifically possible!

> Rising from the dead? That sounds impossible, right? It's hard to make sense of!

Some people think maybe Jesus' followers took His body from the tomb, which is why it was empty. Others say the whole story of Jesus coming back to life was just made up by His followers.

> If it really happened, shouldn't there be proof?

BIBLICAL VIEW

Many history and Bible experts have been curious about what happened on that first Easter. They looked into the facts of Jesus' resurrection. Some of these experts believe in Jesus, while others don't. But they all agree on a few important things:

- The **tomb** where Jesus was buried was **empty**, even though it was sealed and guarded by Roman soldiers. Pontius Pilate, the Roman governor, made sure it was very secure after Jesus was buried (Matthew 27:65–66).

- After Jesus rose from the dead, He **appeared to more than 500 people** all at once (1 Corinthians 15:6).

- Jesus' followers who were once scared or didn't believe in Jesus became really **brave** preachers and leaders after they met the risen Jesus.

We'll explore more proof of Jesus' resurrection later. *(Check out the **Fact Check** section.)* But for now, let's do a fun activity that shows how one incredible event—like Jesus' resurrection—can change many lives!

3-6 Jesus' Resurrection: Fact or Fiction?

Activity

Exploding Sticks Chain Reaction

MATERIALS

- Jumbo wooden craft sticks (at least 25 pieces)

3-6 Jesus' Resurrection: Fact or Fiction?

INSTRUCTIONS

1. This specific chain reaction is called the "cobra weave." To begin the chain, arrange four craft sticks in the pattern shown in the picture, making sure to pay attention to where they overlap.

2. Add another stick *diagonally* across the top to secure the start of the "chain." This stick should hold down the ends of the top horizontal stick and the right vertical stick.

   Tip:

   If the diagonal stick isn't holding the two sticks securely, try sliding them outward until they are firmly held down by the diagonal stick.

3. Add more sticks to the "unsecured" side to make the chain longer. Each stick should go *over* one stick and *under* another stick. Keep your hand on the last stick you added to maintain the chain.

3-6 Jesus' Resurrection: Fact or Fiction?

4. To start the chain reaction, release your hold on the last stick and watch what happens.

109

3-6 Jesus' Resurrection: Fact or Fiction?

Discussion

1. What do you think is the most exciting part of this activity?

   _____
   _____
   _____
   _____

2. Let's find out how the **chain reaction** works!

   The secret behind a chain reaction is two types of energy: **potential energy** (the energy that's stored up) and **kinetic energy** (the energy of things that are moving).

   When we weave the sticks together, it creates **tension**, like a coiled spring. This builds up potential energy, which is just waiting to be released. Then, when we let go of the last stick, all that **stored energy is set free**! The sticks fly through the air as the potential energy turns into kinetic energy, starting the exciting chain reaction!

   *(For more details on these two types of energy, check out the **Fact Check** section.)*

3. Let's talk about the two parts of our chain reaction. The first part happens when we **"build potential"** in the sticks by weaving them tightly—just like winding up a spring.

   Now, think about what Jesus did *before* He died on the cross. How do His life and teachings connect to what we did in our activity? (**Hint:** It has something to do with His disciples.)

   _____
   _____
   _____
   _____

*(**Answer:** Just like we built up potential energy in the sticks, Jesus was preparing His disciples. He healed the sick, taught people, and did miracles. His disciples watched and learned from Him every day. Jesus was **getting them ready with the knowledge and skills** they would need to share His message with others, just like we "**built up**" the energy to make the chain reaction happen.)*

4. The second part of the chain reaction is **"setting it into motion."** What made the chain reaction happen? And what event made Jesus' disciples and followers start going out and spreading the good news about what Jesus did?

   _____
   _____
   _____

*(**Answer:** Releasing the sticks triggered the chain reaction. In Jesus' story, **His resurrection** was the game-changer. The tomb was empty, and He appeared to many people.)*

Before Jesus' resurrection, the disciples were like the tightly wound sticks in our activity—full of potential, but filled with fear after Jesus was arrested and crucified. Peter even denied knowing Jesus three times!

But everything changed when **Jesus rose from the dead**! When the disciples saw the risen Jesus, they were no longer afraid. They were **filled with boldness** and **began to spread the good news of Jesus' resurrection** everywhere. The book of Acts in the New Testament shows their brave adventures as they shared the message of Jesus with the world.

5. How do we tell others why Easter is special for us as Christians? Why is Jesus' resurrection important to us?

(*Answer:* Jesus' resurrection shows God's love and the power of His sacrifice.)

The enemy has been defeated.
Death could not hold Jesus down.
God has won the battle for us.
Our debt has been paid.
And we can be friends with God again.
This is why Easter is such a joyful and powerful celebration for Christians!

6. Even though the devil has been defeated, he still tries to bring us down with him.

> "He prowls around like a roaring lion, looking for someone to devour." (1 Peter 5:8)

So, what can we do about this?

(*Answer:* Let's allow God to equip us as we pray and read the Bible, spend time with Him and His people, and experience His goodness. When we get to know Jesus, our lives will truly change!)

Summary

Jesus rising from the dead shows us how powerful God is. He loves us and forgives our sins. With His resurrection, the **enemy has been defeated** once and for all!

His victory gives us **hope** and **new life**. Get ready to share this amazing news with everyone around you: Jesus is alive!

Truth to Remember

Jesus is alive! Death could not hold Him down. He has won the battle for us.

He was handed over to die because of our sins,
and he was raised to life to make us right with God.

Romans 4:25

FACT CHECK

TWO TYPES OF ENERGY

Energy comes in two main types: **potential** and **kinetic**.

When someone says, "You have a lot of *potential*," it means you can do something you haven't done yet. This is like **potential** energy—energy that's **stored** and **waiting to be used**. For example, a bicycle at the top of a hill or a stretched rubber band has potential energy because it's waiting to move.

On the other hand, **kinetic energy** is the energy of **movement**. It's what happens when the bicycle rolls down the hill, the book falls to the ground, or the yo-yo swings back and forth. All of these things are in motion, using kinetic energy!

EVIDENCE OF JESUS' RESURRECTION

Fact #1: Jesus appeared to many people in person.

The tomb where Jesus was buried was sealed and guarded, but on Easter morning, it was empty! An angel told the women: "*He isn't here! He has risen from the dead, just as he said would happen.…*" (Matthew 28:6). If Jesus didn't rise again, how could so many people have seen Him alive?

Here are some **stories** from the Bible of **people meeting Jesus after He rose**:

- **Mary Magdalene** talked with Jesus on Easter morning (John 20:16-18).
- **Cleopas and another disciple** walked and talked with Jesus on the road to Emmaus (Luke 24:13-31).
- Jesus asked **His disciples** to touch Him so they could see He was really alive. He even said to **Thomas**, "*Put your finger here, and look at my hands. Put your hand into the wound in my side. Don't be faithless any longer. Believe!*" (John 20:27).
- Jesus cooked breakfast for **His disciples** by the sea (John 21:9).
- Jesus gave **His disciples** instructions known as the **Great Commission** (Matthew 28:16-20).
- Jesus appeared to **more than 500 people** during the 40 days before going up to Heaven. (1 Corinthians 15:6).
- The **apostles** saw Jesus go up to Heaven (Acts 1:4-9).

Fact #2: Fearful followers became bold believers.

When Jesus was arrested and crucified, His followers were afraid and ran away. One famous example is **Peter** (Luke 22:7-62).

Before:

At the Last Supper, Peter confidently said, "*Lord, I am ready to go to prison with you, and even to die with you.*" He even tried to protect Jesus by cutting off someone's ear during the arrest. But later, fear took over, and Peter denied knowing Jesus three times!

After:

After Jesus came back to life, He appeared to His disciples. Seeing Him alive made them believe He really was the Son of God, just like He said!

Before going back to heaven 40 days later, Jesus gave them a mission: "*Go and make disciples of all nations*" (Matthew 28:16-20).

With the help of the Holy Spirit, **they became brave and started sharing the good news about Jesus everywhere** (Acts 1:8). These disciples were called **apostles**, which means "ones sent out."

One of the bold apostles was **Peter**. On Pentecost, Peter spoke to a huge crowd, and 3,000 people believed in Jesus and were baptized (Acts 2). He told everyone about Jesus, including non-Jews (Gentiles), and endured suffering, arrests, and punishment for his faith (Acts 5:41).

Tradition says Peter was crucified on Vatican Hill in Rome during Emperor Nero's rule.[2] Because he didn't feel worthy to die like Jesus, he asked to be crucified upside down. Today, St. Peter's Basilica in Rome stands where Peter gave his life for Jesus.

St. Peter's Basilica

Fact #3: Unbelievers had a change of heart after meeting with the risen Jesus.

- **Paul**, once known as Saul, used to dislike Christians. He even hurt and punished them for believing in Jesus. But one day, on his way to Damascus, Jesus appeared to him and said, "*Saul! Saul! Why are you persecuting me?*" (Acts 9:4).

  After meeting Jesus, Paul completely changed. He repented, started believing in Jesus, and traveled far and wide to tell others about Him. Paul's letters to churches became a big part of the New Testament!

- Another example is **James**, Jesus' own brother. At first, James didn't believe in Jesus or His mission (John 7:2-5). But after seeing Jesus alive again, everything changed! James went from a doubter to one of the key leaders of the church in Jerusalem (1 Corinthians 15:7). He even wrote the book of James in the New Testament.[3]

NOTE: For the next lesson, parents can prepare a windmill in advance to show children an example of what they will be making.

3-7

Holy Spirit: Our God and Helper

3-7 Holy Spirit: Our God and Helper

NOTE: Prepare a sample of the windmill before the lesson.

PURPOSE

To introduce the Trinity to children, helping them understand who the Holy Spirit is, why He is called our Helper, and why it's important to be filled and led by the Holy Spirit.

Note: While some people use examples like eggs, water in different states, or clover leaves to explain the Trinity, these illustrations are not entirely accurate. For clarity and accuracy, we will not use them in this lesson.

Icebreaker

- If you could invent something to help you and others, what would it be?

Today we're going to explore one of God's biggest mysteries…the **Trinity**! Have you ever heard of the "Trinity"? Do you know what it means?

The Trinity means that our **God is one**, but He exists **in three different persons**: the Father, the Son (Jesus), and the Holy Spirit. So, God is 3-in-1! Each person is *fully* God, not just a part of God. They all deserve equal praise and worship. Even though they are different, they work together perfectly in unity. It's pretty amazing, isn't it?

· · ·

NON-BIBLICAL VIEW

Some people don't understand how one God can be three persons, and they might say,

"**If you add 1 + 1 + 1, you get 3! That means Christians must be worshiping three different gods,** *not* **one.**"

Others forget about the Holy Spirit, thinking He's not as important as the Father or the Son. Some even think of the Holy Spirit as just a power or force from God, instead of understanding that He is a person and fully God, just like the Father and the Son.

BIBLICAL VIEW

So, does the Bible talk about the Trinity? Let's check out some examples:

- **The Creation story** (Genesis 1:26–27)

    When God created people, He said, "Let **us** make human beings in **our** image, to be like **us**…." Did you notice God used the words "us" and "our"? That shows there's **more than one person** involved.

    But then, it says, "So God created human beings in **his** own image. In the image of God **he** created them." Did you note the shift to "his" and "he"? These words point to **one person**.

    These verses show God exists in more than one person but is also one.

- **Jesus' Baptism** (Matthew 3:16–17)

  When **Jesus** (the **Son of God**) came up from the water, the **Spirit of God** came down like a dove and rested on Him. Then, a voice from heaven (**God the Father**) said, "This is my Son, whom I love." Here, we see all three persons of the Trinity working together.

- **Christian Baptism** (Matthew 28:19)

  Jesus told His disciples to "go and make disciples of all the nations, baptizing them in the name of the **Father** and the **Son** and the **Holy Spirit**."

  Again, we see all three persons of the Trinity are mentioned as *equally important*.

· · ·

Some things about God are beyond our understanding. Deuteronomy 29:29 reminds us that God has secrets we can't fully know. It's like trying to solve a puzzle without all the pieces!

There will always be some things that remain a mystery because we, as humans, are limited in our understanding.

We worship a God who is mysterious and beyond our understanding. Sometimes we may struggle to find the right words to describe Him. The Trinity is one of those mysteries. Instead of trying to figure it all out, we can trust and obey a God we can't fully describe. It's something worth thinking about.

When someone says the Trinity doesn't make sense because of the math, you can tell them that there's more than one way to look at it. Instead of adding, try multiplying: **1 x 1 x 1 = 1**.

Now, let's talk about the third person of the Trinity: the Holy Spirit. Some people call Him the "Holy Ghost" or the "Spirit of God." But whatever name you use, remember that **the Holy Spirit is just as important as God the Father and Jesus.**

The Bible says the Holy Spirit was involved in creation (**Genesis 1:1–2**):

> In the beginning God created the heavens and the earth. The earth was formless and empty, and darkness covered the deep waters. And **the Spirit of God was hovering over the surface of the waters**.

So, the Holy Spirit has been present since the very beginning!

While Jesus was on Earth, He made a promise to His disciples. He knew He wouldn't stay on Earth as a human forever. So, He asked His Father to send a **Comforter** and **Helper** who would always be with us (John 14:16–17). Can you guess who the promised Helper is? It's the Holy Spirit!

The Holy Spirit will lead us into all truth and will never leave us alone. What a great promise!

Today we're going to make a paper windmill and test it to lift things up. Let's get started! (**Optional:** If you have a sample windmill, you can show it and talk about some interesting facts about windmills.)

3-7 Holy Spirit: Our God and Helper

Have you ever seen a windmill before? Do you know what it does and how it works?

A **windmill** is a tall structure with large blades or sails that can spin when the wind blows. Inside, there are gears and machinery that use the spinning blades to help do different tasks. Some things windmills can do are:

- grind grains to make flour
- press seeds to make oil (for example, olive oil)
- drain water from wetlands
- cut wood
- chop up hay
- lift water from wells
- make electricity, and more!

3-7 Holy Spirit: Our God and Helper

Activity

Paper Windmill

NOTE: *You can either make one windmill per person, or work together as a family to make one windmill*

MATERIALS

- Construction or cardstock paper (or thin cardboard from a cereal box)
- Cardboard tube (from the middle of paper towels, or make one from construction/cardstock paper taped together to form a tube)—*one for each windmill*
- A straw—*one for each windmill*
- Pushpin or small nail
- Sharp pencil
- Ruler
- Scissors
- String
- Tape
- Small cup *(optional—to test the windmill)*
- Small, light objects that can fit inside the cup, for example, rice, paper clips, or small erasers *(optional—to test the windmill)*
- A glass of plain milk *(optional—for discussion #5)*
- Chocolate syrup *(optional—for discussion #5)*

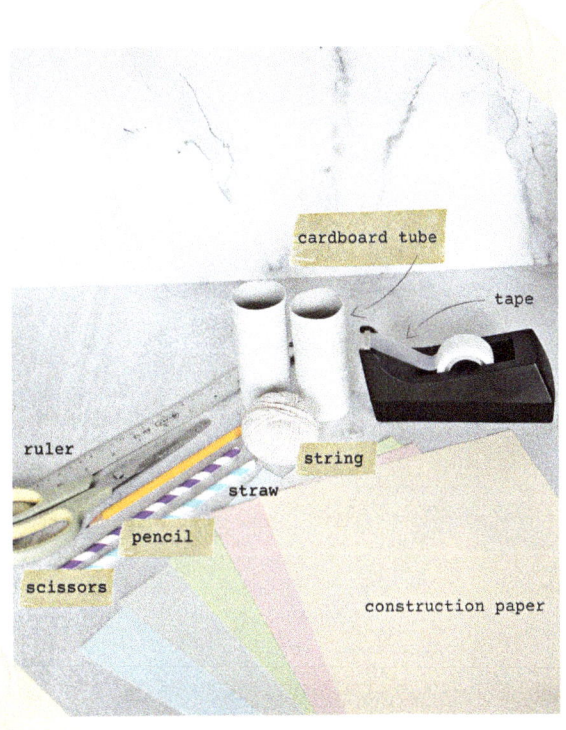

127

3-7 Holy Spirit: Our God and Helper

INSTRUCTIONS

1. Cut a square piece of construction or cardstock paper with each side measuring 8 inches.

2. Draw a vertical line and a horizontal line down the middle of the square, making four smaller squares (4 inches on each side.

3. Cut 2-inch slits along the lines on all four sides of the large square.

4. Fold every other side up toward the middle of the square to create sails for your windmill.

5. Use a sharp pencil to poke a small hole in the center of the square. The hole should be just big enough for a straw to fit snugly.

Tip:

If the straw is thinner than the pencil, start by making a hole with a pushpin or small nail. Then, gently twist the straw into the hole to widen it slightly.

6. Push the straw through the hole. Make sure the paper sails move together with the straw when you turn them. If the hole is too big, use tape to make it smaller.

7. Set aside the straw and paper sails.

8. Use a pushpin or small nail to make two holes opposite each other at the top of a cardboard tube.

9. Enlarge the holes slightly with a pencil. These holes need to be *bigger* than the straw so it can fit and turn loosely later.

10. Push the straw with the paper sails through both holes in the cardboard tube. Test if the straw can turn smoothly by blowing on the sails.

11. Your paper windmill is done! Now, let's test it out.

    Blow gently on the windmill from different directions—front, back, sides, and top. You can also try using a hairdryer or fan to blow air on it.

12. See how fast or slow the sails turn based on how strong the wind is.

13. **Optional:** Test how the windmill can lift things:
    - Tie a piece of string to the straw *behind* the sails and tube. Tape the string to make sure it stays securely attached to the straw.
    - Tie a small cup to the other end of the string.
    - Place some small, light objects inside the cup.
    - Blow on the windmill sails and see how much the windmill can lift. You can also try using a blow dryer for a stronger airflow.
    - Experiment with different weights of objects. See how hard you need to blow to lift them up!

3-7 Holy Spirit: Our God and Helper

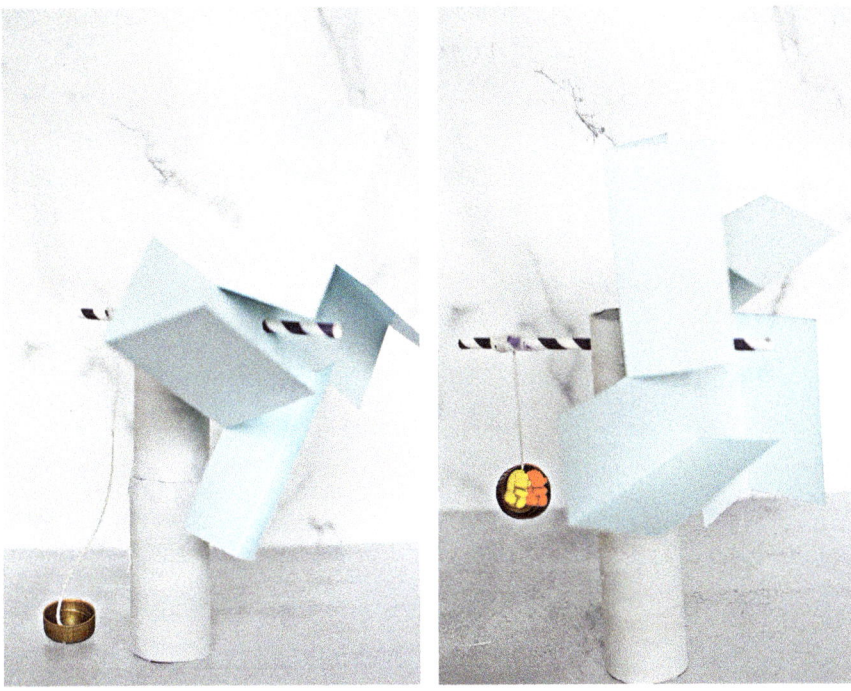

ENGINEERING NOTES ABOUT THE PAPER WINDMILL:

- The wind pushes against the folded edges of the paper sails, causing them to spin.
- As the sails spin, the string wraps around the straw, lifting the cup with the small objects inside.
- Windmills work best when they are facing the direction the wind.

Did you know that real windmills in northwestern Europe can be turned to face the wind?

This is important because the wind can change directions there. People who take care of windmills have to move the sails so they face the wind and work properly.

3-7 Holy Spirit: Our God and Helper

Discussion

1. What did you learn about the windmill? What makes it work?

   _____
   _____
   _____
   _____

   (Answer:
   - *It needs wind to work. The wind is what powers the windmill.*
   - *It has to face the wind to work well.*
   - *The stronger the wind, the faster the sails turn, and the more the windmill can do.)*

2. Let's imagine that the "wind" in our activity is like the Holy Spirit, and the "windmill" represents us. Can the windmill work without the wind?

   Just like the windmill needs wind to work, Christians need the Holy Spirit to help us live and do what God wants.

3. How can we tell if we have the Holy Spirit in us? (**Hint**: Read Ephesians 1:13)

_____

_____

_____

(**Answer:** *When we believe in Jesus as our Lord and Savior, we receive the Holy Spirit.*)

Ephesians 1:13 says, "And **when you believed in Christ**, he identified you as his own by **giving you the Holy Spirit**, whom he promised long ago."

The Bible also says we are **God's holy temple** (1 Corinthians 6:19). The Holy Spirit lives inside of us!

4. Jesus said the Holy Spirit is our **Helper**. How does the Holy Spirit help us?

(**Note:** *The following list provides the answers with Bible references. You can review the main points now and explore the Bible verses later.*)

He **comforts** us when we are sad or scared. We can have peace and joy, knowing God is with us.	**1 Corinthians 6:19** "Don't you realize that your body is **the temple of the Holy Spirit**, who **lives in you** and was given to you by God? You do not belong to yourself." **Romans 14:17** "For the Kingdom of God is not a matter of what we eat or drink, but of living a life of **goodness** and **peace** and **joy in the Holy Spirit**."
He **helps us remember and understand** what we learn about God.	**John 14:26** "…the Holy Spirit—he will **teach** you everything and will **remind** you of everything I have told you." **Isaiah 11:2** "And the Spirit of the Lord will rest on him— the Spirit of **wisdom and understanding**, the Spirit of **counsel and might**, the Spirit of **knowledge** and **the fear of the Lord**."

3-7 Holy Spirit: Our God and Helper

He **helps us pray**, even when we don't know what to say.	Romans 8:26 "And the Holy Spirit **helps us in our weakness**. For example, we don't know what God wants us to pray for. But the Holy Spirit **prays for us** with groanings that cannot be expressed in words."
He **shows us when we've done something wrong** and helps us make it right. When we feel bad about something we've done, it's the Holy Spirit helping us understand it was wrong.	John 16:7–11 "…And when he comes, he will **convict the world of its sin**, and of God's righteousness, and of the coming judgment" (v. 8).
He **guides us to grow** and **do what's good**.	Romans 8:14 "For all who are **led by the Spirit of God** are children of God." Galatians 5:22–23 "But the Holy Spirit produces this kind of **fruit in our lives:** love, joy, peace, patience, kindness, goodness, faithfulness, gentleness, and self-control. There is no law against these things!"

5. Ephesians 5:18 says we should "**be filled with the Holy Spirit**" every day. What does it mean?

   *(**Note:** You may demonstrate the following illustration to the kids. You will need a glass of milk and chocolate syrup.)*

   _____

   _____

   _____

   *(**Answer:** Although the Holy Spirit lives inside us when we believe in Jesus, sometimes we forget to let Him lead our lives.)*

3-7 Holy Spirit: Our God and Helper

Let's imagine your life is like a glass of plain milk, and the Holy Spirit is like chocolate syrup. When you believe in Jesus, the Holy Spirit is poured into your life—just like the syrup in the milk.

But if you don't mix it, the syrup just stays at the bottom. That wouldn't taste very good, right? We need to stir the syrup (the Holy Spirit) into the milk (our life) to enjoy it fully!

6. How can we be filled with the Holy Spirit?

_____

_____

_____

(**Answer:** We can **pray** to the Holy Spirit every day, **asking for His help and guidance**, especially when we have to make decisions.

We also need to **listen to His voice** and **obey** Him, which helps us make good choices and avoid sin. The more we let Him lead, the more He helps us grow and do good things in our lives, blessing others along the way.)

Summary

The Trinity means God is **one**, but He **exists in three persons**: the Father, the Son (Jesus), and the Holy Spirit. Each one is fully God and deserves our praise and worship equally.

The Holy Spirit is our **Comforter** and **Helper**, promised by Jesus to always be with us. We need to live each day filled with and led by the Holy Spirit.

Truth to Remember

There is only one true God, existing in three Persons: the Father, the Son Jesus Christ, and the Holy Spirit.

The Holy Spirit is my God, my Helper.

For all who are led by the Spirit of God are children of God

Romans 8:14

FACT CHECK

WHY DO PEOPLE THINK OF THE WIND WHEN THEY THINK OF THE HOLY SPIRIT?

In the Bible, the words used for "**Spirit**" also mean "**wind**" or "**breath**." In Hebrew, the word for Spirit is **ruach**, and in Greek, it's **pneuma**.[1] Both words suggest something unseen but powerful, like the wind. For example, Moses said, "O Lord, you are the God who gives **breath [ruach]** to all creatures…" (Numbers 27:16).

In John 3, Jesus compared the Holy Spirit to the wind when speaking with a Pharisee named **Nicodemus**: "The **wind** blows wherever it wants. Just as you can hear the wind but can't tell where it comes from or where it is going, so you can't explain how people are born of the Spirit" (John 3:8). This helps us understand the mysterious nature of the Holy Spirit, who moves in ways we can't always see or explain.

However, while the Holy Spirit is like wind—unseen and powerful—He is *not* just a force. The Holy Spirit is God Himself, equal with God the Father and God the Son.

HOW ELSE DID THE HOLY SPIRIT APPEAR IN THE BIBLE?

The Holy Spirit also appeared as a **dove** during Jesus' baptism and as **tongues of fire** during the first Pentecost (Acts 2:1-13), showing His presence and power in different ways.

Here's a list of all Truths to Remember and the memory verses from this book for a quick reference and reminders. The powerful Truths in these pages will help your family stand up against the enemy's lies. The Bible says to "repeat them again and again." Talk about them when you are at home, on the road, going to bed, and getting up (See **Deuteronomy 6:7**). You may create a memory card for each Truth and Bible verse, ask children to write the Truths in their journals, or have a quick quiz during car rides.

1
My greatest gift is this:
Jesus died on the cross to save me from my sins.

> …and the blood of Jesus, his Son,
> cleanses us from all sin.
>
> —1 John 1:7

2
I am saved by God's grace, not by my works.
God's grace is enough for me.

> My grace is sufficient for you,
> for my power is made perfect in weakness….
>
> — 2 Corinthians 12:9 (NIV)

3   Jesus Christ is real. He was a part of history, and I want Him to be a part of my story too.

Then Jesus told him,
"You believe because you have seen me.
Blessed are those who believe without seeing me."

— *John 20:29*

4   Lord Jesus became fully human to save us completely.
He truly is a wonderful Savior!

This High Priest of ours understands our weaknesses,
for he faced all of the same testings we do, yet he did not sin.

— *Hebrews 4:15*

5   On the cross, Jesus died as a perfect sacrifice to pay for our sins.

He personally carried our sins in his body on the cross
so that we can be dead to sin and live for what is right.
By his wounds you are healed.

— *1 Peter 2:24*

6 Jesus is alive!
Death could not hold Him down.
He won the battle for us.

> *He was handed over to die because of our sins,*
> *and he was raised to life to make us right with God.*
>
> —Romans 4:25

7 There is only one true God, existing in three Persons:
the Father, the Son Jesus Christ, and the Holy Spirit.
The Holy Spirit is my God, my Helper.

> *For all who are led by the Spirit of God are children of God.*
>
> — Romans 8:14

For family:
Does your family cherish God's gift of salvation every day, or just on Christmas or Easter? Here are some ways to make it a daily treasure: spend time each day with the Gift-Giver in prayer and by reading His Word, give thanks in all situations, live in a way that honors Him, and trust that His plans always lead to our ultimate good.

For parents:
Parents, remember that God always keeps His promises. Trust that He will fulfill His promises for our children too. We are not alone in this journey of parenthood. The Holy Spirit, our promised Helper, is here to stay with us. He is our wisest friend, guide, comforter, intercessor, and above all, our God. What do you need today to navigate this journey of parenthood? Psalm 27:14 encourages us, "Wait patiently for the Lord. Be brave and courageous." God's grace is *always* sufficient.

Notes

Unless otherwise noted, all websites were last accessed on 1/6/2021.

3-1: The Greatest Gift

1. Stephen Juan, "What Are the Most Widely Practiced Religions of the World?" *The Register*, 6 Oct 2006, www.theregister.com/2006/10/06/the_odd_body_religion/.

2. Hillary Morgan Ferrer, "Ever Wondered What Other World Religions Actually Teach?" *Mama Bear Apologetics*, March 25, 2018, mamabearapologetics.com/what-world-religions-teach-intro/.

   In this blog post, Hillary Morgan Ferrer interviewed Lindsey Medenwaldt about her series on major (or well-known) world religions and how they are different from Christianity. Find the series here: mamabearapologetics.com/category/world-religions/.

   Some that were already published are Christianity, Judaism, Jehovah's Witness, New Age Movement, Progressive Christianity, and Islam. There are two main articles per religion. The first will focus on similarities and differences between the world religion and Christianity. The second will be in a "frequently asked questions" format. It will deal with the most common questions children have about the other religion.

3. "Kaihōgyō," *Wikipedia, The Free Encyclopedia*, last revised on January 29, 2021, en.wikipedia.org/wiki/Kaihōgyō.

3-2: Amazing Grace

1. Lee Strobel, *Case for Grace for Kids*, (Grand Rapids, MI: Zonderkidz, 2015), 77–80.

3-3: Jesus Christ: Fact or Fiction?

1. "Gospel (n.)," Online Etymology Dictionary, www.etymonline.com/word/Gospel.

   The word gospel comes from the Old English word "godspel": "god" means "good," and "spel" means "news, story, message."

2. Lucy Olofinjana and Catherine Butcher, "What People in England Think of Jesus, Christians and Evangelism," *Talking Jesus*, p. 5 and 11, talkingjesus.org/wp-content/uploads/2018/04/Talking-Jesus-dig-deeper.pdf.

   The adult research was carried out in 2015 by Barna Group and ComRes. Barna Group is a visionary research and resource company located in Ventura, California. For the young adult research, ComRes interviewed two thousand people aged eleven to eighteen online between December 7–19, 2016. Data were weighted to be representative of this audience by age, gender, and region.

3. "How Many Prophecies Did Jesus Fulfill?" Got Questions Ministries, January 2, 2020, www.gotquestions.org/prophecies-of-Jesus.html.

4. "44 Prophecies Jesus Christ Fulfilled," Roman Catholic Church of St. Thomas More, Swiss Cottage Parish, November 2014, parish.rcdow.org.uk/swisscottage/wp-content/uploads/sites/52/2014/11/44-Prophecies-Jesus-Christ-Fulfilled.pdf.

5. Simon Gathercole, "What Is the Historical Evidence that Jesus Christ Lived and Died?" *The Guardian*, April 14, 2017, www.theguardian.com/world/2017/apr/14/what-is-the-historical-evidence-that-jesus-christ-lived-and-died.

6. Christopher Klein, "The Bible Says Jesus Was Real. What Other Proof Exists?" *History Stories,* February 26, 2019, www.history.com/news/was-jesus-real-historical-evidence.

7. Flavius Josephus (circa 93), *The Antiquities of the Jews* (William Whiston, Trans.), book XVIII chap. 3, Project Gutenberg, gutenberg.org/files/2848/2848-h/2848-h.htm

8. "Evidence for Jesus," All About GOD Ministries, www.allaboutarchaeology.org/evidence-for-jesus.htm.

9. Biblical Archaeology Society Staff, "The House of Peter: The Home of Jesus in Capernaum?" *Bible History Daily*, February 7, 2020, www.biblicalarchaeology.org/daily/biblical-sites-places/biblical-archaeology-sites/the-house-of-peter-the-home-of-jesus-in-capernaum/.

3-5: The Cross: Fact or Fiction?

1. Sarah Pruitt, "Died Like Jesus? Rare Remains Suggest Man Was Crucified 2,000 Years Ago," *History Stories*, June 4, 2018, www.history.com/news/jesus-christ-death-crucifixion-archaeology.
2. "Crucifixion Evidence," All About GOD Ministries, www.allaboutarchaeology.org/crucifixion-evidence-faq.htm.
3. "Evidence for Jesus," All About GOD Ministries, www.allaboutarchaeology.org/evidence-for-jesus.htm.
4. "Garden of Gethsemane," All About GOD Ministries, www.allaboutarchaeology.org/garden-of-gethsemane-faq.htm.
5. "Pontius Pilate," All About GOD Ministries, www.allaboutarchaeology.org/pontius-pilate-faq.htm.
6. "Caiaphas," All About GOD Ministries, www.allaboutarchaeology.org/caiaphas-faq.htm.
7. "Church of the Holy Sepulchre," All About GOD Ministries, www.allaboutarchaeology.org/church-of-the-holy-sepulchre-faq.htm.

3-6: Jesus' Resurrection: Fact or Fiction?

1. Andreajn, "Easter Facts," Facts.net, March 8, 2020, facts.net/history/religion/easter-facts.
2. Daniel William O'Connor, "St. Peter the Apostle," Encyclopaedia Britannica, February 19, 2020, www.britannica.com/biography/Saint-Peter-the-Apostle.
3. Jack Zavada, "What Is the Book of James About?" Learn Religions, August 25, 2020, learnreligions.com/book-of-james-701033.

3-7: Holy Spirit: Our God and Helper

1. "Hebrew Roots/Trinity/Holy Spirit," Wikibooks, March 15, 2020, en.wikibooks.org/wiki/Hebrew_Roots/Trinity/Holy_Spirit.

Photo Credits

Welcome to Bible Comes to Life!
Joy Sukadi

3-1: The Greatest Gift
Creative Nina/Shutterstock
Karolina Grabowska/Pexels
Azmat1/Shutterstock
Paul shuang/Shutterstock
Jantanee Runpranomkorn/Shutterstock
Tokoamanjaya/Freepik

3-2: Amazing Grace
Nes/iStock
Jackson David/Unsplash
Premium AI/Freepik
Boonyachoat/iStock
Emma Bauso/Pexels

3-3: Jesus Christ: Fact or Fiction?
artplus/iStock
Kara Gebhardt/iStock
Jaflippo/iStock
Cecilie_Arcurs/iStock
Premium Photo/Freepik
Klug-photo/iStock
Free Wind 2014/Shutterstock
Jojan/Wikipedia
LexiJoy/Flickr
Berthold Werner/Wikipedia
Capernaum/Holy-land-tours
beachlovernc2015/Tripadvisor
May Thawtar/Adobe Stock
Sinhyu Paphayom/iStock
Jill Wellington/Pixabay

3-4: Jesus Christ: Fully God, Fully Man
kipgodi/Shutterstock
Voortman Photography/Shutterstock
Greyson Joralemon/Unsplash
Omar Amar/Shutterstock
RyanJLane/iStock
Wirestock Creators/Shutterstock

3-5: The Cross: Fact or Fiction?
Ross Gordon Henry/Shutterstock
AXP Photography/Pexels
ZU_09/iStock
Arthit_Longwilai/iStock
Dmitry Pistrov/Adobe Stock
AlexDonin/Shutterstock
Anton_Ivanov/Shutterstock
NOWAK LUKASZ/Shutterstock

3-6: Jesus' Resurrection: Fact or Fiction?
Romolo Tavani/Shutterstock
JESHOOTS.COM/Unsplash
Jill Wellington/Pixabay
RomoloTavani/iStock
Jasper Boer/Unsplash
AleksandarNakic/iStock
S.Borisov/Shutterstock

3-7: Holy Spirit: Our God and Helper
Soloviova Liudmyla/Shutterstock
Robo Wunderkind/Unsplash
MarioGuti/iStock
Luan Souza/Shutterstock
Ground Picture/Shutterstock
mcclainashanti/Shutterstock
Sabir Benghaline/Shutterstock
Savvas Kalimeris/Unsplash

Truth Blast!
Joy Sukadi

All Activities
Joy Sukadi

About the Authors

Joy Sukadi is a wife, mom of three, and a passionate preacher of God's Word. She has mentored and taught Jesus to women in her community in the past twenty years. She is currently pursuing a Theology Degree at Portland Bible School. Joy also runs a photography business and sees this as an opportunity to connect with local moms. In her spare time, she loves to bike with her family, hike the beautiful Pacific Northwest, do arts and crafts, and play games with her kids. She can't live without Jesus, coffee, and a series of good books.

Lilyana Margaretha is a wife and mom of two girls. She is passionate about equipping Christian parents on how to raise their kids with a biblical worldview. She has a doctoral degree in Molecular and Cellular Biology from the University of Washington. She has a vision of connecting science and the Bible, making it logical, relevant, and applicable in children's lives. Lilyana loves to make crafts, do science with her kids, and enjoy the beauty of the Pacific Northwest with her family.

www.ingramcontent.com/pod-product-compliance
Lightning Source LLC
Chambersburg PA
CBHW061119070526
44583CB00028B/3341